STAND OUT

7 steps to self-publishing a book that will **build your profile, promote your business** and **make you stand out from the crowd**

Michael Hanrahan

First published in 2014 by
Michael Hanrahan Publishing
PO Box 319
Surrey Hills 3127

© Michael Hanrahan 2014
The moral rights of the author have been asserted

All rights reserved. Except as permitted under the *Australian Copyright Act 1968* (for example, a fair dealing for the purposes of study, research, criticism or review), no part of this book may be reproduced, stored in a retrieval system, communicated or transmitted in any form or by any means without prior written permission. All inquiries should be made to the author.

National Library of Australia Cataloguing-in-Publication entry:

Author:	Hanrahan, Michael.
Title:	Stand out: 7 steps to self-publishing a book that will build your profile, promote your business and make you stand out from the crowd / Michael Hanrahan.
ISBN:	9780992291754 (paperback)
Subjects:	Self-publishing – Handbooks, manuals, etc.
	Electronic publishing.
	Authorship – Marketing.
	Publishers and publishing.
Dewey Number:	070.593

Printed in Australia by McPherson's Printing
Text design by Michael Hanrahan Publishing (www.mhpublishing.com.au)
Cover design by Peter Reardon (www.pipelinedesign.com.au) and Michael Hanrahan

10 9 8 7 6 5 4 3 2 1

Disclaimer
The material in this publication is of the nature of general comment only, and does not represent professional advice. It is not intended to provide specific guidance for particular circumstances and it should not be relied on as the basis for any decision to take action or not take action on any matter which it covers. Readers should obtain professional advice where appropriate, before making any such decision. To the maximum extent permitted by law, the author and publisher disclaim all responsibility and liability to any person, arising directly or indirectly from any person taking or not taking action based on the information in this publication.

Contents

Foreword   1
Preface   3

PART I: THE 7 STEPS

Step 1: Planning   13
Step 2: Editing   33
Step 3: Design   57
Step 4: Proofreading and indexing   69
Step 5: Printing   73
Step 6: The ebook   91
Step 7: Distribution   101

PART II: AFTER YOUR BOOK IS PUBLISHED

Using your book in your business   111
Other stuff   125
Appendix: your questions answered   129
Glossary   135
Index   141

Thanks to...

...Anna, for everything

...Mum, Brigid, Sheena, Archie and Lik for being awesome, all the time

...Lesley Williams, Geoff Wright and Greg Brown, for teaching me 87.3 per cent of what I know about publishing and printing

...Peter Reardon, Charlotte Duff and John Peter, for their excellent assistance with design, editing and proofreading

...the KPI gang, who helped make this happen, especially Andrew Griffiths and Team Awesome

...Dad, who's not here to see this but whose contribution was invaluable just the same.

About Michael Hanrahan

After completing a Post Graduate Diploma in Writing and Editing at Deakin University, Michael started his publishing career at Wrightbooks, the leading publisher of business, finance, property and investment books in Australia for over 20 years. There he held the roles of editor and production coordinator. When Wrightbooks was taken over by John Wiley & Sons in 2001, Michael took on the role of Managing Editor, managing a team of editors and overseeing the production and publication of 50 to 60 books per year.

Michael left John Wiley & Sons in 2004 to start Michael Hanrahan Publishing Services, offering writing, editing and self-publishing services. Due to his background, Michael attracted many authors looking to self-publish a book they had written to promote themselves and their business. Michael Hanrahan Publishing Services recently became Michael Hanrahan Publishing, and now focuses on providing self-publishing services for authors who have written a book for their business. Having held various roles in this area, Michael is confident that he has worked on more titles in this particular niche than any editor in Australia.

Having worked in the industry for 17 years and grown up with a writer father, Michael has seen more of the publishing world than most. He has never stopped to count how many books he has been involved with but it's comfortably in the hundreds. In 2011 he started small press Rough Draft, which has to date published four books, with two more in the works at the time of writing.

Michael has worked with many best-selling authors across many different subject areas – including small business, finance, health and fitness, real estate, law, investment, self-help and travel – and has seen time and again how writing a book can launch or boost a business. He was recently asked by the highly regarded KPI program to give a talk on self-publishing for business.

"I've relied on Michael Hanrahan's eye for detail and editing skills since 1997. There is no-one who is more capable, more focused or more dedicated than Michael when it comes to every aspect of the publishing game. As a best-selling author, I feel I'm in a position of authority to judge who is brilliant and who is a complete waste of time in the publishing industry. For every one of your self-publishing needs, Michael is your man."
Louise Bedford, author of four best-selling books on the sharemarket, www.tradinggame.com.au, Melbourne

"Michael helped me take my book from a Word document to a professional business tool, the perfect 'business card', that has opened up new opportunities and seen my business grow. In *Stand Out* Michael helps self-publishing authors navigate the many paths that lead to a published book. As he did with me, Michael guides readers through his seven steps of self-publishing, explaining in an accessible yet in-depth style – without jargon but with subtle humour – how you can create a powerful business tool in the form of a book. His experience, professionalism and personable nature shine through!"
Russell Newman, author and self-publisher of *The New CEO in You!*

"When becoming an author the whole process can be a little daunting. Michael Hanrahan took me under his wing and showed me the way. Always there to answer questions so I was reassured about the whole process. Michael edited with precision and care and made me feel included in the process. I would highly recommend his editing and self-publishing services to anyone considering becoming a first-time author."
Clare Balmer, brand designer, author and self-publisher of *Expandable Brands*

"Michael helped with the editing, layout and production of my book, and in the process helped me improve it a lot. From the moment I first spoke to Michael it was clear that he is a self-publishing expert and that he would ensure my book looked great and was of a professional standard. I would highly recommend Michael for all small business self-publishers."
Ned Coten, author and self-publisher of *Game Plan Marketing*

Foreword

Writing and publishing a book is a powerful way for a businessperson to build their profile and increase their credibility. Even today, with blogs, websites, Facebook and Twitter, a printed book still has an air of authority that sets a published author apart from the crowd. I've worked in this area of publishing for many years in various roles, and I've seen firsthand the opportunities that can come from publishing: speaking engagements, interviews, articles, reviews, new clients and partnerships – the list goes on and on.

Self-publishing a book can provide an excellent return on your marketing dollar. But it is an extension of you and your brand so it must be a quality product. You have taken the bold move to publish your story so why wouldn't you publish the very best book that you can? Unlike blogs and Tweets, your book will be around – either in print or digitally – for years. It is vital that you get it right. *Stand Out* will help you do just that.

Ten or fifteen years ago it was very complicated, expensive and time-consuming to self-publish a book, but not anymore. Technology today makes it easier to produce books. Improved digital printing means smaller print runs are more affordable and better quality, desktop publishing software packages make it easier to design and produce books, and the internet is a global marketplace where authors and publishers can promote and sell their books. Sounds great! Anyone can be an author. The flip side is everyone can be an author, so how can you stand out?

One way would be to learn from Michael Hanrahan's extensive publishing experience that he freely shares in this book.

The message that comes across clearly in *Stand Out* is that there is no secret to publishing. But there is a process that Michael goes through in plain English. All areas of publishing are covered: from editing, to typesetting, printing and distribution and the all-important marketing and promotion. The explanations are clear and concise and Michael's anecdotes, gleaned from working with hundreds of authors over his career, brought a wry smile to my face on several occasions as I read the manuscript.

Although Michael has worked in the industry for years, he has the ability to step outside and look in at the publishing process through the eyes of those encountering our world for the first time. He demystifies what can seem quite strange to those working on a book for the first time.

I would imagine that most people reading this book will be considering writing a book of their own or have completed their manuscript and are wondering, 'Where to now?' Well, you have arrived at the right place.

I congratulate Michael on writing this excellent handbook – an essential guide to self-publishing for small business.

Lesley Williams
Founder, Major Street Publishing

Preface

The phone call ...

Let me tell you about a phone call I receive a few times a week.

The phone rings, and of course I stop what I'm doing and answer it, as long as the cat isn't sitting on my lap or the dog isn't in the way and I can actually get to the phone. After cheerful greetings, the person on the other end tells me they've written a book. They launch into an explanation of who they are and what their book is about, usually becoming quite enthusiastic. This lasts for about 10 minutes. At the end of the explanation they pause and take a deep breath ... and then they ask:

'What do I do now?'

I've heard this question so many times, and it's what I'm going to answer in this book. This is probably where you're at right now; excited about the prospect of getting your book out there but a little unsure of how to go about it. You've probably done some research on the internet, and discovered lots of information is freely available about how to self-publish a book (some of it great and some of it not so good). This book is going to take you from start to finish through the process, from having your manuscript assessed, to editing, layout and covers, through to printing, bookshop distribution and ebooks.

Why self-publish a book for your business?

Writing a book as a business tool is a growing trend that has been spurred on by two significant developments in book publishing. First is the rapid advances in the publishing industry that have made self-publishing more accessible for small businesses. The key changes include ebooks, retail sites such as Amazon, and low-cost, high-quality short-run printing. These technology-related changes give independent publishers the ability to produce and distribute (to a worldwide audience if desired) high-quality books. Ten years ago self-publishing was much more expensive and the results weren't nearly as good. There weren't many people or businesses around who specialised in this area, and it was often seen as a form of publishing used by people whose books weren't good enough to be accepted by a 'real' publisher. It was often derisively called 'vanity' publishing – a term that is rarely heard these days.

The second development is the rise of the high-profile entrepreneur, with Richard Branson being a prime example. Self-promotion (rather than just promoting a company) has become a powerful tool in modern business, aided by social media and traditional media that love such stories. People such as Branson, Steve Jobs, Dick Smith, Oprah Winfrey, Mark Zuckerberg and Janine Allis have become household names, and are often as well known as their companies, if not more.

Preface

I have worked in this area of publishing for a long time, and in the last couple of years have seen a rapid rise in the number of authors deciding to go it alone – for a number of different reasons – rather than go with a traditional mainstream publisher.

So what's in *this* book?

To put things into context before we go any further, you need to know about two assumptions I make throughout this book.

First, I assume you have either finished writing your book for your business *or* that you're considering writing one and want to learn more about self-publishing. Either way, you're looking for advice on what happens *once you have finished the writing process*. You can find many good books that will help you develop your idea for your book and assist with the writing process itself; this isn't one of them.

Secondly, I assume that you're aiming to produce a *professional-quality book*. All sorts of guides on the internet can tell you 'how to produce your book for little or no money' by 'doing it all yourself'; for example, by 'doing your own editing and layout in Microsoft Word' and then uploading your files to one of the free ebook sites. While this is technically possible, it's not going to produce a professional-standard book. And plenty of resources will tell you how to 'sell a million copies on Amazon' – but we all know a formula to such things doesn't exist. If it did, the person who wrote the book would open a publishing company, not put these so-called secrets in a book. If you're after a cheap and quick way to produce your book, this guide is not for you.

So let's have a look at what you'll find in these pages.

The Seven Steps

Over the years at Michael Hanrahan Publishing we've refined our process into a seven-step self-publishing system that's logical and easy to follow. Part I of this book is based on this seven-step system, with some additional information for self-publishers who wish to manage the process themselves. The steps make it easier for self-publishers to understand the process, and also ensure that things are done at the right time and in the right order. Whether you're managing the process yourself or using a self-publishing company, you too can follow these steps:

1. **Planning:** this step looks at working out a schedule and planning your budget, and who you need to help you with your book if you are managing the process yourself.

2. **Editing:** during the planning stage, you can determine what level of editing is required. (You'll learn all about the different levels of editing in these pages.) It is my experience that while by the end of the editing process authors realise their book has been greatly improved, at the beginning first-time authors are often a bit daunted. They can be unsure about having somebody look closely at their work. To help you understand the editing process and what to expect, I explain how a book is edited, what role the editor plays and what the self-publisher (that's you) has to do.

3. **Cover and interior design:** creating a book cover that looks good, and is inviting and easy to read, is very important. This part of the book also addresses the interior layout.

4. **Proofreading and indexing:** once the design and edit are wrapped up, the book is indexed and proofread.

Preface

5 **Printing:** it's very helpful for self-publishers to know a little about the printing process. This step looks at the different printing options available, how many copies to print, digital versus offset printing, printing in Australia versus offshore, unit cost and more.

6 **The ebook:** you need expert help to produce a professional-standard ebook. This section addresses the different file types, uploading, and the more limited formatting options of ebooks.

7 **Distribution:** many bookshops don't like dealing with self-publishers who only have one book. I explain why you should consider using a distributor and the advantages of doing so, and what you need to do if you want to go it alone.

In Part II, I take you through what to do after your book is published:

- I examine publicity and using your book to promote your business. Most authors who publish in this area don't aim to make money from book sales – they aim to make a profit by generating increased business. I cover how to prepare a media release and a media list appropriate for your book, and how to approach the media. *Stand Out* also explains other ways to use a book to promote a business, such as giving away copies to potential clients, arranging speaking engagements on the topic of the book and giving away sample chapters on a website.

- I look at the little things you need to do after your book is published that many authors overlook, such as sending copies to the national and state libraries.

At the end of the book you will find a section answering commonly asked questions and a useful glossary. Throughout the book I also introduce you to some terms used in publishing; knowing what these mean will be helpful for you when dealing with people in the industry.

How to stand out ...

So why is this book called *Stand Out*?

While more and more books are being self-published by entrepreneurs, business owners and experts in their fields, the vast majority of people still haven't written and published a book – and that includes your competitors. So getting your book out there will make you and your business stand out. If you create a professional-standard book and promote it well, this will separate you and your business from the other businesses in your industry. It will make you stand out as an expert and as an authority in your field, and your business will benefit accordingly. I know lots of editors and publishers – I'm the only one who has written a book about self-publishing. The fact that you're reading this book right now makes me stand out from my competitors, and that's what you'll achieve with your book.

The other way to make yourself stand out from the crowd is to publish a *professional-standard* book. Reading this book is a great step in that direction. While the number of books being self-published has grown dramatically in recent years, many are still poor quality. Designers and printers with basically no experience with books are jumping in to make a buck; editors with little or no experience with the complete publishing process are trying to produce books. An author came to me recently who had used a

Preface

self-publishing company to produce his first book. This company had done – frankly – a very poor job. With this book he had just glimpsed the potential of being a published author, but he knew his books didn't represent him and his business very well. The day after I sent him samples of some of the books we've produced, he rang me and basically said, 'I don't care how much it costs, just do my book like that!' He knew what a powerful tool a book could be, but he also knew the finished product needed to be executed to a high standard or it would actually have the opposite of the intended effect – making his business look cheap and amateur.

Self-publishing a book is not just a great thing to do for your business, it is also an exciting and fun process. While it's also a lot of work – and you need to be ready for that – it's very rewarding. I've worked with scores of authors who have seen great benefits to their businesses through having a book published. This book is a practical tool that will help you join them. I'm going to give you a comprehensive and honest look at what's involved. I'm not going to give you the fantasy of selling a million copies on Amazon while producing your book for $13.00. Like anything you do in business there are some risks and potential pitfalls, and we'll look at those too. If you inform yourself and enlist the right help, these can almost always be avoided.

I wish you well on your self-publishing adventure.

Michael Hanrahan
May 2014

PART I

THE 7 STEPS

Planning

As with any major project, planning is crucial – that's why it's Step 1 in our seven-step system.

In this chapter I start by looking at the various publishing models, to help you understand what you're getting into when you self-publish. Knowing where you fit in the publishing spectrum will help you navigate the process and make better decisions. Then I get into the details of planning your publishing project.

The three different publishing models

'I'm working on a book…what do I do when it's finished?' I love it when I'm asked this question by authors. It's often the very first step in what becomes an exciting project and enjoyable relationship with the author. The first thing I do when I'm asked this question is ask the author what stage they're at with their book; that is, have they finished writing it, are they halfway through, have they completed a first draft? This helps me establish what type of help they might be after.

The next thing I do is explain to authors what the different publishing options are. People usually call me looking for help with self-publishing, but I find giving them a bit of an overview of how the publishing industry works helps them understand the self-publishing process, and I also like to make sure authors understand and have considered all the options before they proceed. So, although this book is about self-publishing, I run through the other publishing models here to help you understand the differences, and the advantages and disadvantages (yes, there are some!) of self-publishing.

These days, different publishing permutations and combinations are appearing all the time. The industry has changed rapidly in recent years and the lines between the different publishing models are now sometimes a little (or a lot) blurred. I regularly speak to authors and publishers who have bent and twisted the book model to suit their needs, often successfully but sometimes not. Still, you can publish a book in three basic ways – all other methods are based on these, and they're what we'll look at now.

Traditional publishing

Traditional publishing is the form of publishing most people are familiar with. In traditional publishing an established publishing company – big, such as Penguin, or small, such as Sleepers (one of my favourite small publishers) – finds a book that they think they can make profitable. The book has to be high quality and marketable, and the publisher must be satisfied that they can work well with the author. They then negotiate a contract with the author and – if a contract is agreed upon – take on production of the book. The publishing company is responsible for paying all the costs and managing the publication of the book, and shares the profits with

Step 1: Planning

the author in the form of a royalty payment, usually around 10 per cent of the recommended retail price of the book.

The key advantages of this approach for authors are they don't have to pay anything to have their book published and they get expert editing, design, printing, marketing and distribution. In exchange for this, the author gives much of the decision-making over to the publisher and shares the profits.

People who advocate self-publishing often state that in working with a traditional publisher you 'give up control of your book' and that this is a major drawback, but this sort of argument is deliberately not giving you the full story. Yes, you do 'give up control of your book' to some extent, but you do that because the publisher is paying the bills, not you. You can't expect somebody else to pay to produce your book but let you make the final decisions. If you're a control freak, traditional publishing is probably not for you.

Another common issue often raised is that self-publishing is better because you get to 'keep all the rights in your book'. This issue is usually raised by people trying to sell you self-publishing services, and once again it's deliberately a bit misleading. In a standard contract with a traditional publisher, you retain all the rights in your book but *licence* them to the publisher, usually for a defined period of time. This licence includes some restrictions on what you can do, such as not publish a 'competing work' for a certain period of time, or on how you can use the material in the book. Any restrictions placed on the author are commensurate with the time, money, effort and skill the publisher has contributed to the project. Once again, they're paying the bills so you cede some control to them. This is reasonable and only to be expected. (I think too much promotion of self-publishing revolves around excessively criticising traditional publishing – you won't find any of that here.

While the majority of my work is with self-publishers, I also run a traditional publishing company – Rough Draft – that we started a few years ago.)

One thing to note, however: if you're ever presented with a contract that asks you to assign full rights to the publisher, run away as fast as you can. Unscrupulous operators exist in every industry, including books, and unfortunately some unwitting authors have handed full rights to publishers and been mortified at the results, only to realise they have no recourse because they didn't fully understand their contract. Everybody in the publishing industry has heard such a horror story or two, but this usually happens to uninformed authors who are desperate to see their work in print. No respectable publisher wants to take full rights in your work.

Self-publishing

Self-publishing is where the author also takes on the role of the publisher, usually with the assistance of an editor or a self-publishing company. The greatest single advantage of self-publishing – and the reason many authors choose this route – is that it guarantees your book gets out there. The biggest hurdle to traditional publishing is simply that many, many more manuscripts are written than books published every year. My small press, Rough Draft, has published four books in three years at the time of writing, and in that time I've received a few hundred manuscript submissions for consideration. It's the same everywhere. As such, many good books are regularly knocked back by publishers because the resources simply aren't available to publish them all. If you have the time, money, energy and enthusiasm, with self-publishing you can avoid this significant drawback of traditional publishing. You're not dependent on finding somebody else to support your book to get it out into the world.

Step 1: Planning

With self-publishing, the responsibility for the book lies completely with the publisher (which is also the author, which is you). You have the final say on every decision, and many authors self-publish precisely to have this control. (Note that you have this control because *you* are paying the bills; traditional publishers have the control because *they* are paying the bills.) By working with a skilled self-publishing professional, you can still get the expert assistance you need *and* make all the decisions yourself. If you want a fluorescent hot-pink cover with green typography and gold embossing on your name, your publishing professional will probably tell you it's a bad idea, but then you get to make the final choice. (I do have to caution you, though, that if you go against the advice of your publishing professional too often you will probably end up with a substandard book.) From a decision-making point of view this can be the best of both worlds; hire a good company to help you and you get expert advice but still get to make the decisions.

But there's no such thing as a free lunch; with all the decision-making power comes all the financial risk of the project. Although this can be managed with good advice, as with any business project it's never eliminated. Realising that as a self-publisher you're taking on all of the business risk of the book is very important. This is the definition of what a publisher does, whether it's you or Sleepers or Penguin. You may have an editor, or designer, or self-publishing company help you produce your book, and they will support and advise you as best they can. But, ultimately, the success or otherwise of the book rests entirely with you.

Partnership publishing

Partnership publishing is an area where inexperienced authors can get caught out. It's a hybrid model, somewhere between traditional publishing and self-publishing. Nothing is inherently wrong with the partnership publishing method, and it can produce excellent results, but it does open up unwary authors to being ripped off. The 'partnership' is formed by the publisher signing up the author to what is much like a traditional publishing contract, but also asking the author to contribute to the costs of the book or to commit to buying a large number of books from the publisher, or both.

Like anything in business, if the terms of the agreement are reasonable and the risks and returns for the publisher and author are equitable, partnership publishing is fine, and can be very successful. A good friend of mine runs her publishing company this way; she is very successful with many happy authors.

Where authors can run into trouble with this model is if they're unaware of where the risks and rewards lie. With traditional publishing, the author contributes the time and energy to write the book, the publisher contributes the money and skill to publish and distribute the book, and the profits (or losses) are shared. Shared risk, and shared reward. All good. With self-publishing, the author contributes everything and keeps all the profits (or losses). All the risk, and all the reward. All good again. But a dodgy partnership publishing deal hands most or all of the risk to the author but then shares any rewards with the publisher. That's not good at all.

This happens because the publisher asks the author to 'contribute', say, $10,000 to the project. The book is then produced cheaply and this amount covers most – if not all – of the production costs. So the author has unknowingly paid for the book to be produced. But the author is then paid a royalty on sales, thus sharing the profit with the publisher. If the book doesn't sell well, the publisher hasn't really lost anything because the production costs were

Step 1: Planning

largely or completely covered by the author, but if it does sell well, the publisher shares in the success. The worst of these stories are of authors paying $10,000 or $15,000 – or even more – to get 100 copies of their book poorly produced, and receive marketing that consists of the book being listed on a website and put in a brochure, and that's about it.

Fortunately these stories seem to be rarer these days. The changes in the publishing industry have made self-publishing very attractive, and mountains of information about publishing is now easily available, so the opportunities to take advantage of uninformed authors are disappearing. If you ever have the opportunity to get involved in partnership publishing, do your homework and read the contract very carefully. It's great if done well, and a potential disaster if not.

So, you've decided to self-publish ...

You're reading a book about self-publishing for small business so I'm going to take the small leap and guess that you've decided to stand out from your competitors and self-publish a book for your small business. The preceding brief overview of the other options has hopefully helped you understand a bit more about where you fit into the publishing landscape, which I think is very important. I'm now going to give you a quick overview of what's involved in self-publishing your book, and then cover the process in detail using our seven-step system.

It's not all beer and skittles

Let's get this out of the way first: a lot of work is involved in self-publishing a book. Anybody who tells you it's easy is probably trying to sell you something. Even with the help of a self-publishing expert, you still have to be heavily involved every step of the way, and you have final responsibility for all decisions. You'll be involved in editing, layout, cover design, printing, the ebook, publicity and distribution. The process usually takes three to six months. And once your book is published, you then have to promote it and sell it. For most self-publishers, this is something they have to fit in around the other work they're already doing, which for a small business owner is likely to be a lot.

If you're not up for this commitment, self-publishing is not for you. But ask yourself this: when was anything that was really worth doing easy? The reason most people haven't written and published a book is that it takes commitment and effort. You will stand out from your competitors when your book is published because you'll be recognised as the person who had the dedication and wherewithal to complete something most people only talk about.

It's not free

You will have to put some money into your book to get it produced properly, but you need to see this as an *investment* rather than a *cost*. If you publish your book to a professional standard and use it well in your business, it will more than return your investment, usually many times over. Most projects I work on involve an investment of around $5000 to $10,000, though I've had two projects in the last six months that have been over $20,000 and another that was over $15,000. The biggest variable expense in a self-publishing project is the printing; with one of those $20,000-plus projects, the author printed 2500 copies – a large run for a self-publisher – and with the other the author printed in full colour.

Step 1: Planning

And keep in mind this is just the investment to produce the book. Publicity and marketing can easily cost another $2000 to $5000, or even more.

It's great for your business

Okay, so that's the hard stuff. Now let's look at the good stuff.

Being a published author will help you build your profile, promote your business and make you stand out from the crowd. It's a turbocharged business card, a demonstration of your skill and experience, an ad, a marketing tool, a symbol of your commitment to seeing a project through, a key that will open many doors, a representation of the standards of your business.

I speak to authors all the time who tell me how having a published book has brought all sorts of benefits to them and their business. I spoke to one author recently who had very carefully tracked sales related to his book, and after about six months he put the value of extra sales at over $50,000 and growing rapidly. I can guarantee that if you produce a high-quality book and use it well in your business, tangible results will emerge in your bottom line. I've seen it time and time and time again.

I examine in Part II how you can use your book to boost your business.

It's very rewarding

I have *never* worked with an author who held their printed book in their hands at the end of the project and said, 'You know what, I really wish I hadn't done this.' And usually it's the exact opposite – first-time self-publishers are almost jumping up and down with excitement when their book arrives from the printer. On that day

I feel like their new best friend. As well as being a very powerful business tool, writing and self-publishing a book is a great personal achievement and something to be very proud of. Many a bottle of champagne has been drunk when books first arrive. (I *love* that day.)

It's a lot of fun

Yes, time, effort, discipline and financial investment is involved, but every author I work with thoroughly enjoys the process. Yes, all of them. In publishing a book you learn a lot about a whole new industry. You get to meet and work with interesting, creative people. And at the end of it you have a book you can be proud of. I've been involved with hundreds of books in my life, and I've enjoyed every single one. And I still get excited at the start of a new project and a buzz when the books arrive from the printer. I know you'll love it too.

Planning your project

By now you should be getting an idea of what's involved in self-publishing, so we're going to get started on Step 1, the practical aspects of planning your totally awesome book.

You need to think about three key areas before your project can commence:

- Who is going to help you put your book together?
- What is your schedule for your book?
- What is your budget for your book?

Step 1: Planning

Assembling your self-publishing team

You need a number of people to help you put your book together. First I'm going to address the individuals you can hire if you're going to manage the publishing process yourself (being your own project manager), and then I'm going to look at using a self-publishing company to help you out. These companies can take care of all your needs in one stop, providing all the services you need and managing the project for you.

DIY self-publishing

If you're going to manage your publishing project yourself, you'll usually require:

- An editor and proofreader: the next step looks at editing in detail, and how to find a good editor. If you're managing the project yourself, keep in mind that you need an editor *and* a proofreader. Your editor cannot proofread your book because the role of the proofreader is to check for mistakes, and your editor won't usually pick up any mistakes they may have made themselves.
- Designer: for your cover and your interior layout.
- Printer: obviously!
- Bookshop and ebook distributor.
- Ebook converter (or your designer might be able to help with this).

With a bit of time and effort you can track these people down. You might be able to get some recommendations from friends, family or colleagues, and these individuals or companies will all have websites or be members of peak bodies that manage databases and contact details. Keep in mind that it's best to find people or companies with experience working on books. For example, I've seen things go very wrong when designers who haven't worked on books before have tried to do an interior layout. And printers that don't regularly print books can produce sub-par results. So when you're assessing a potential service provider, ask them about books they have worked on and to see some sample copies if possible.

Self-publishing companies

The other option, rather than finding the members of your self-publishing team yourself, is using a self-publishing company to help you. This means that, rather than having to locate and manage five or six people to help on your book, you'll have (usually) just one person coordinating the whole project for you. You'll still be involved in all the decisions, but managing all of these service providers will be taken off your hands.

These days you can choose between quite a few such companies. Some offer a complete range of services, including ebooks and distribution; some can help you write your book as well; some specialise in certain areas of publishing. It's helpful to know what services you need before you start looking, but if you don't, ring up the companies you're considering and ask them. It's part of their role to advise you on what services you need to produce a professional-quality book.

If you select this option, as with choosing any service, shop around until you find a self-publishing company you feel you can work with. Ask them to send samples of books they have worked on recently. Tell them what your book is about and what you plan to do with it, and then ask them for their advice. Most such companies will be happy to spend some time with you to explain how they can help. If a company isn't willing to have a chat and give you some information, it's probably not the sort of company you want to be working with anyway. We give free, no-obligation, 30-minute phone consultations to potential clients. Often we end up working with these people, but sometimes we don't and that's fine too. If I've given somebody some information that will help them with their book, I'm happy.

Should you manage the process yourself?

So should you project manage the process of publishing your book yourself or find a self-publishing company to help you? Both approaches have advantages and disadvantages, and I've seen great books and not-so-great books produced both ways. Project management is an important part of the publication of your book. It involves:

- arranging and monitoring the schedule for your book
- creating and overseeing a plan for everything that needs to be done for your book to be published
- finding and liaising with service providers, such as designers, editors, proofreaders, printers and indexers
- making sure things are done in the right order
- getting quotes and paying the bills.

If you're well organised, prepared to put in the time and effort, and are enthusiastic about doing something new, you can manage your project yourself. I've certainly seen some great books produced this way and the authors have found it challenging but manageable and exciting. Think of it like managing a renovation on your house. You can find the architect, the electrician, the plumber, the carpenter and all the other people you need yourself, or you can find a building company that will take care of the whole thing for you.

An advantage of managing your project yourself is that you can shop around and find the lowest cost designer, editor, printer and so on. The trade-off, as with most things, is that in *possibly* saving a few dollars you'll have to put in a lot more effort yourself, both in finding people to help you and then in managing the project yourself. Coordinating everything takes a lot of time, and it can be difficult to make sure everything happens on time and in the right order, especially for your first book.

The other option is to find a self-publishing company that not only provides the services you need but also manages the whole process for you – a 'one-stop shop'. This has a number of advantages:

- you only have to deal with one service provider throughout the publication of your book

- you have somebody to guide you at every step of the way, explain what you need to do and what your options are

- the process often runs more smoothly because the self-publishing company has systems in place to manage and coordinate the different stages of the process

- you won't have to worry about the more mundane tasks of publishing your book, such as purchasing an ISBN and barcode.

Step 1: Planning

Most will help authors with developing their manuscript, through editing, layout and printing, proofreading and indexing, to ebook formatting, and some offer bookshop distribution as well. Many won't help you write your book but will help you refine it once it's written.

If you take up the full package, a full-service company might also actually provide lower cost services when compared to doing it yourself, because managing the whole process introduces efficiencies that can save you money (and time). For example, editing a book can also include some preliminary work on the formatting. At Michael Hanrahan Publishing, if we edit the book and are also providing the layout, we can prepare the book for our formatting systems during the editing stage. If the person editing your book doesn't know the systems and requirements of the person doing the design and layout, this can introduce some inefficiencies, with the designer at times having to undo and then re-do some of the preliminary formatting work done by the editor. A lot of technical issues need to be managed in producing a book, so having everything done in one place can be advantageous. So you may actually find little or no cost advantages in shopping around for individual services.

Scheduling

You will need to work out a schedule for your book. Often the best way to do this is to work out when you need books by and then work backwards. (See Step 7, later in this book, for more on book launches and when your book should come out.) If you don't have a specific launch date planned, work out when your manusript will be ready to start the publishing process and use the following timelines to work out when your book will be ready.

Here are some general guidelines for how long you can expect each step to take, based on a 40,000-word book that doesn't require a heavy edit or a complicated layout:

- *First edit:* three to four weeks.
- *Internal design and layout:* two to four weeks.
- *Second edit:* one to two weeks.
- *Cover design:* two to four weeks (alongside edit and layout).
- *Proofreading:* one to two weeks.
- *Indexing:* one to two weeks.
- *Printing:*
  - Black-only interior printed in Australia: two to four weeks.
  - Full-colour interior printed offshore: two to three months.
- *Ebook formatting:* one to three weeks.
- *Ebook uploading:* one to two weeks.

These steps and processes are all addressed in this book.

Keep in mind the following when considering these timelines:

- All steps are done sequentially except for the cover, which is a stand-alone process and is usually done in parallel with editing and interior layout, so the cover doesn't usually require extra time that you have to factor in.
- The timelines will vary if your requirements differ. For a book of 40,000 words being printed in Australia, expect the whole process to arrive at the printed book to take two to three months (or maybe a little bit more), with a few extra weeks for the ebook. If your book is, say, 100,000 words, expect three to four months for the printed book.

Step 1: Planning

- You have to be heavily involved every step of the way – the preceding suggested timelines are dependent on you being readily available during the publishing process and you keeping things moving. Often with self-publishing the biggest hold-up is from the self-publisher, because they're trying to fit production of the book in around their day job, which is already keeping them busy.

- These timelines are for guidance only. Every editor, designer, proofreader, self-publishing company and so on will have their own processes and schedules. Make sure you discuss this with them when you're investigating suppliers to ensure they can meet your required deadlines. If you need your book turned around quickly, you may be able to negotiate an express service for an extra fee.

And here's a very important tip for you: if your book launch is on 15 April, don't work out a schedule that gets books delivered to you on 14 April. There are two reasons for this:

- The first is obvious: if any delays occur, you'll have a launch without a book! It happens! Things can and do get held up. Maybe you thought you could get permission to use an extract from another book, but when it was turned down you had to do some rewriting. Maybe the printer discovered a problem with your files. And then there's the unavoidable speed bumps in life: maybe your editor gets sick and needs to take a week off, or you do. For this reason, I always like to build at least two weeks extra into a schedule between books being printed and the launch. Once when I was working at John Wiley & Sons, due to an extremely tight schedule I picked books up from the printer at about 6 pm and drove directly to the launch – which was at 7 pm. This is not advisable.

- The second reason is that if you're distributing your book through bookshops, you need to allow time for stock to filter out to stores. Any publicity you get for your launch will be largely wasted if no books are available for people to purchase. It takes a few weeks for stock to be sent out and placed on shelves, so keep this in mind.

Budgeting

As with anything in your business, thinking carefully about how much money you're prepared to invest in publishing your book is important. Keep in mind that if you do it well, you can really make your business stand out and the financial rewards can be great. Skimping on the production costs of your book can backfire – a poor-quality book isn't going to make you or your business look good or stand out. In fact, the exact opposite will happen: it will make you look like you do things by halves.

To help you decide how much to invest in your book, have a think about what it will be worth to your business. If you sign clients up to $5000 contracts, you only need to sign a few clients to cover the cost of your book, and that's usually easily done. If the value of each of your clients is lower, have a think about the publicity the book is likely to generate and the business it will drive. An ad in a magazine can cost $10,000. Would a book generate more publicity? For sure. You only need to get one article or review about the book in that same or a similar magazine to receive the same coverage, and then you still have all the other things you can do with the book.

Step 1: Planning

To help you work out how much you will need to invest in your book, following are some indicative costs for a 40,000-word book. As with the earlier scheduling information, services and options will differ with different suppliers, but this information will help point you in the right direction. The costs I've provided cover the range for what you can expect to pay to have your book produced by an experienced professional. You might be able to find a former English teacher who will 'edit' your book for $400 – that's not what we're interested in here. Nobody can edit a book properly for $400.

All of the following issues are covered in this book, and all figures include GST. So let's have a look:

- *Manuscript assessment (optional):* $500 to $1000.
- *Developmental edit (optional):* $500 to $2000.
- *Copyedit:* $1600 to $3200. Will be at the lower end if you write well and have worked on your manuscript a lot before sending it to the editor.
- *Interior layout:* $1600 to $3200. Will be at the lower end if your book is mostly text. Will be at the higher end if you have many different styles of text or lots of images, tables, diagrams and the like.
- *Cover:* $400 to $1000.
- *Proofreading:* $600 to $800.
- *Indexing:* $600 to $1500.
- *ISBNs:* Free to about $50 each, depending on the supplier you use.
- *Barcodes:* Free to about $50 each, depending on the supplier you use.

- *Printing:* Giving a price range on printing is very difficult because there are so many variables, but here are some sample specifications and some indicative prices. These specifications are very common for a business book.

  Format: A5
  Pages: 200
  Cover board: 300 GSM[1]
  Full-colour cover with gloss lamination
  Text paper: 80 GSM
  Black-only text (internals)
  Perfect binding[2]

  100 copies: $700 to $1300
  200 copies: $1300 to $2200
  500 copies: $2200 to $3500
  1000 copies: $3500 to $4500

Please use all of these prices as a guide only. Many variables are involved in the process of producing a book and the investment required by you will vary accordingly. As with anything, you will also pay according to the level of skill and experience of the service provider you are using; expect to pay less for an editor who has been in the game for just a few years and more for an experienced professional who has 20 years of experience. When you speak to a service provider, they will be able to provide you with costs for your book after some discussion with you and looking at your manuscript.

---

1 GSM measures grams per square metre and relates to the weight of the paper. Usually, the higher the GSM, the thicker the paper.

2 'Perfect' binding is the most common form of book binding. Just about every book on your shelf will be bound this way. Just think of it as 'standard' binding.

Editing

How many times do you think I've heard an author say this: 'My book was better *before* it was edited?' If you guessed absolutely never, well done. I've been doing this for over 15 years and that has *never* happened. I did once have a first-time author ring me up and berate me when I returned his edited file because he thought I'd butchered his book. A few days later, after he'd actually been through what I'd done, he sheepishly called back to apologise. He thought the editing was excellent and he was very pleased. So, it's never happened.

Mostly editors get the opposite response. I've lost count of the number of excited authors I've had on the other end of the phone after I've sent their edited book back to them. They ring up and express great surprise at how much an edit has improved the book. Many realise that while they thought their book was good before, the editing process has helped it reached its full potential.

What *is* editing anyway?

Most people who have never been involved in a book have no idea whatsoever about what the editing process involves. They often think the author does all the work and the editor comes in at the last minute and moves a few commas around.

Yes, we check the spelling and the grammar and the punctuation and make sure it reads good...sorry, well...but there's a lot more to it than that. I've had an author dump a pile of barely collated material on my desk – the pile included some pages he'd bashed out between meetings and some notes written on a napkin – as he asked me to turn it into a book. That's fine. It's doable. It's just going to cost more. And I have another author who I work with regularly who is the consummate professional writer; if I have to insert a comma every few pages, I'm surprised. So editing can take many forms, but let me tell you what it will *always* do: it will always make a book better.

But do I *really* need an editor?

Authors sometimes ask if they *really* need an editor. Their arguments usually go something like this:

- 'My spelling is really good, and I've read through the manuscript lots of times. I don't think it needs an edit.' Editing is *much more* than just fixing the spelling.

- 'My Mum reads a lot and she's read it for me. I don't think it needs an edit.' If Mum's not an editor, the book still needs an edit. An English teacher is not an editor. A person who reads a lot is not an editor. The person who writes your website at work is not an editor. Only an editor is an editor.

- 'I've edited it myself.' A lot of the slightly dodgy material on the internet trying to promote cheap self-publishing talks about how you can 'edit your book yourself'. (I saw on one website recently a discussion on 'self-editing'.) Technically this is true; you could edit your book and you'd certainly save yourself a few dollars. You could also give yourself open heart surgery with a bottle of tequila, a Swiss army knife and a sewing kit, but would you really want to?

Even people who are excellent editors can't properly edit their own work. Do you think I edited *Stand Out* myself? Of course not. My wonderful editor, Charlotte, has certainly helped me improve this book. A crucial part of the editing process is getting an expert second opinion on what you've done, and you can't really give yourself a second opinion on your own work. A person who edits their own work has a fool for an author.

So, I've hopefully convinced you that you do absolutely, 100 per cent, without doubt, need an editor. It's non-negotiable if you want to produce a professional-quality book, and I know you do because you're reading this book and not one of the slightly suspect websites that tells you how to produce your book for only $13.00 and sell a million copies on Amazon. Your book will be a reflection of you and your business; you want it to be the best it can be, right?

The role of the editor

Many first-time authors become a little nervous at the thought of somebody editing their book, but there is absolutely no need. The editor is on your side, and is just as keen to publish a good book as you are. It's not like at school where your work is being graded!

A good editor will be very involved with both you and your book, and will be just as enthusiastic about it as you are. Far from just 'correcting' your work, an editor will improve it in many ways small and large, while working with you to ensure you are producing the book that you want.

Your editor will fix up spelling mistakes, inconsistencies, incorrect grammar and other errors, but a good editor will do much more than this. A good editor will:

- suggest additions where more information is required
- suggest deletions where you've included something unnecessary or repeated something
- alert you to any possible copyright concerns
- discuss with you changes that will improve your writing.

Because you're self-publishing, you have the final say in what goes in your book, but you would be well advised to take the advice of your editor in most instances. If your editor has made a change that you don't agree with, raise it with him or her and discuss it. You'll usually find you can come to an agreeable solution and, if not, it's up to you what to do. That's one of the advantages (and occasionally disadvantages) of self-publishing. (If you're publishing through a traditional publishing company, the editor or publisher usually has the contractual right to insist on changes, although in practice this rarely happens and agreeable solutions are almost always found.)

Just the facts, ma'am

It's a common misconception that your editor will check the facts in your book. This is definitely not the case. As both author and publisher it is absolutely your responsibility to get the facts right. It is very important that you're aware of this. If you're writing a book, you are the expert in your field and know more about it than most, and certainly more about it than your editor. So, when you're writing, make sure you're thorough and do your homework. Check your facts. If you put London in the US or start writing about World

Step 2: Editing

War V, your editor will probably notice, but beyond that it's up to you. You can't expect your editor to know that when you wrote 'use a 15 mm spanner' you really meant 'use a 25 mm spanner'.

One exception applies here: you can hire an editor who is an expert or highly experienced in whatever you're writing about and ask them to check the facts, but this is a very big job and will cost you extra, possibly quite a bit. A better option can be to have a trusted colleague who knows your topic review the book for you before sending it to the editor. Most people will be happy to be involved and will do this kind of technical review for a bottle of wine and a free copy of the book.

The importance of finding an editor or company you can work with

Your editor will play a very important role in the final quality of your book. Not only do they need to be highly skilled and to understand your aims for the book, but you also need to get on well with them. You will be working closely with them for a number of weeks (and maybe months).

With this in mind, talking to at least two or three editors or self-publishing providers about your book before selecting somebody, and even meeting with them if you can, is a good idea.

One of the first things I do when I get that first call from an author is ask them to email the book to me so I can have a look. This does two things: it allows me to provide an accurate quote, and it also gives me the opportunity to discuss the book with the author and advise them on what I think needs to be done. I usually ask them to give me a few days to look at it so that I can discuss the book with them properly. Any decent editor or self-publishing company will be willing to do this with no commitment or cost. After you've discussed your book with a few editors or self-publishing companies and received quotes, you'll be able to make a decision on who you think will be best for you and your book.

Although some editors specialise in certain areas, you don't necessarily need an editor who knows your topic well. Any good editor will be able to help you with your book, unless it's highly specialised and requires a detailed understanding of the topic. In all my years editing I've only ever knocked back a couple of manuscripts because the material was highly specialised and I didn't think I was the best person for the job. If this is the case for your book, hunt around until you find the right person and expect to pay more for your edit.

The editing stages

So, now that you've called Mum and told her, 'Sorry, you're not allowed to edit my book', let's have a look at what a *real* editor can do for you.

There are four different stages of editing, though not every book will need every one. The stages are:

- manuscript assessment
- developmental editing
- copyediting
- proofreading.

Copyediting and proofreading *are essential for every book*, but not every project requires a manuscript assessment or developmental editing. After having a look at your manuscript, your editor will be able to advise you on what it requires.

So let's see what's involved in each stage of editing.

Step 2: Editing

Manuscript assessment

A manuscript assessment is when an editor reviews your book and advises you on what improvements can be made. The editor will not usually make any changes to the text, but will instead provide feedback in the form of a written report, which can be anywhere from two to ten pages, or more. Some editors will also make notes in the manuscript, suggesting changes.

Many authors don't have a manuscript assessment done. They're most commonly used by authors who are submitting their book to a publisher and would like to improve the book as much as possible before submitting. Self-publishing authors can use an assessment to receive some expert feedback while they're still working on their manuscript.

In my experience around 20 to 30 per cent of authors submitting to a publisher have an assessment done, and it's fairly uncommon for self-publishing authors. Still, it's an option you should be aware of. Receiving some expert feedback at the end of your second or third draft can be helpful, and then you can do another draft or two. It's not usually worth getting an assessment done after only your first draft because the book will still need work. Better to tidy it up more yourself before you pay for an expert opinion.

If you're going to have this done, many manuscript assessment agencies are available – just do an internet search. A good tip is to have the manuscript assessment provided by somebody other than the editor who is going to copyedit your book – that way, your copyeditor can give you a fresh opinion. Having a manuscript assessment performed may allow you to avoid a developmental editing stage, because in some ways they are similar – they both look at the overall macro issues of your book.

Developmental editing

The editing process proper begins with a macro view of the content of your book, called a developmental edit (or sometimes a structural edit). This is where the editor reads your book and provides feedback on the content and overall structure.

A developmental edit is usually done in Microsoft Word, although it can be done on hard copy as well. Your editor will read your book and provide feedback such as the following:

- highlighting where your book may benefit from additional information
- pointing out any repetition
- suggesting re-ordering, addition or removal of chapters
- suggesting any significant areas of text that could be removed.

Editing at this stage is done on a macro scale, looking at chapters and moving, adding or deleting significant portions of text. At this point, your editor will not be focusing on spelling, grammar, punctuation and the finer details of your book, although the editor may make some corrections here and there. Further refining, adding, moving and deleting will often be done at the copyediting stage as well.

In my experience, about 5 to 10 per cent of books need substantial developmental editing. I worked on a book recently that came to me at 150,000 words. The author had basically just written down everything he could think of on his topic and vaguely arranged it into a book. We went through four rounds of development and ended up with a very well structured 100,000 words. We moved chapters, deleted repetition, added some case studies, and rearranged his various sections, parts and chapters into a more coherent form.

Step 2: Editing

I find that about 30 to 50 per cent of books need some level of development editing when they come to me, and the remainder go straight to the copyediting stage. Keep in mind that your book may still require some rearranging during copyediting, but not usually major surgery. If just very minor developmental work is required, this is often combined with the copyediting.

Copyediting

This is where your editor will start to focus on the text in a bit more detail. By this stage you should have the basic content and structure sorted out, either after a manuscript assessment, developmental edit or simply because your manuscript was in good shape to begin with.

I'm going to outline here how we work with our authors; while every editor works a bit differently, the process you go through will generally be similar whoever edits your book.

The first edit

The things your editor will be looking at during the first edit of your book are:
- consistency of spelling and styles
- improvements to suggest
- clarity of the writing
- spelling and grammar
- basic fact checking.

In the first edit of your book, your editor is going to look at structural issues as well as the more detailed copyediting. If your book needed substantial developmental work, you will probably have had a developmental edit done (see preceding section), but some fine-tuning of the structure and content are still usually required at the copyediting stage.

Most likely, your editor will provide your first edit in Microsoft Word. One of the best things to happen to editing in recent years is on-screen editing. Microsoft Word is very bad for layout but, funnily enough, as a word processor it's very good for…word processing! Most editors these days use Word and its excellent 'track changes' feature.

With track changes turned on, *every single change* the editor makes is highlighted in the file. This is the strength of tracked changes. In the old days, an edit was done on hard copy. The editor would make changes and then highlight the more comprehensive changes for the author to check. This was both laborious and not ideal because, while the author could easily see the highlighted major changes, not all of the smaller changes were marked, which meant the author had to read the book very carefully to make sure they were happy with everything. Even a comma in the wrong place can change the meaning of the text, but an author checking, say, 250 pages could easily miss this.

With tracked changes turned on, the author and editor can see every single space, comma, letter and word that has been moved, added or deleted, which means both can be confident they can see exactly what the other has done. Even when using track changes, your editor may still highlight and explain some changes.

It's up to you to go through this file very carefully and check what has been done. You'd usually be well advised to take on board most, if not all, of the changes made by your editor. I find that most authors accept about 80 to 90 per cent of the changes we make, and sometimes more. From time to time I have an author who doesn't

Step 2: Editing

even return the edited file to me – they just email back and say, 'Fantastic – I accept everything you've done'.

When the file with tracked changes comes back from your editor it will look something like this:

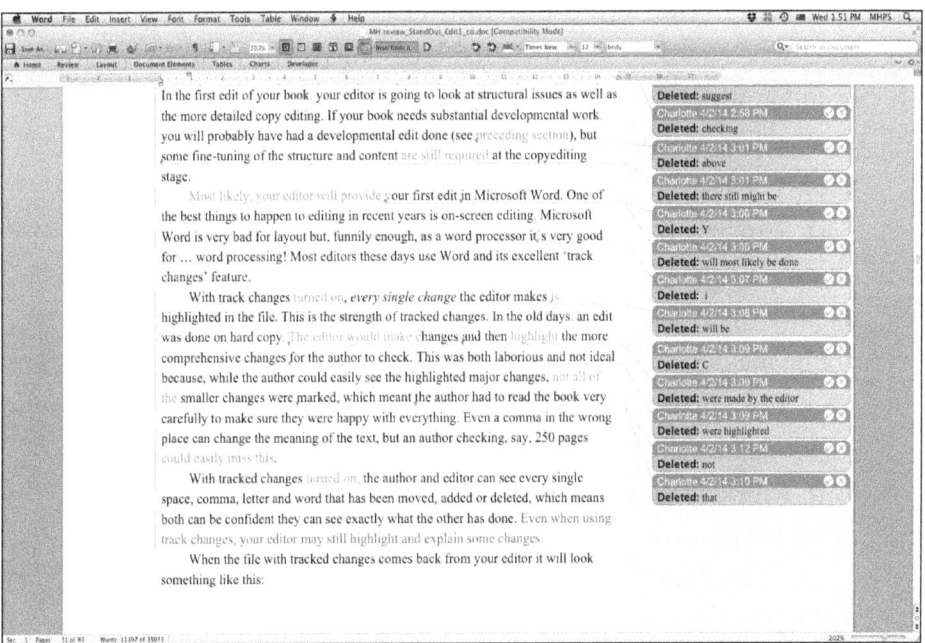

As well as suggested changes, your editor might have some queries for you. For example, they might not have understood something and be asking for clarification, or suggesting some additional text or you move a heading, sentence or paragraph.

When you receive the edited file from your editor, you have another chance to go through your book, making changes in response to your editor's suggestions and queries, or perhaps based on something you've been thinking about yourself. This is usually your last chance in the process to make significant changes, although keep in mind that if you start making too many changes you will probably be charged extra by your editor because you may be undoing work they've already done and they'll have to check the new material.

The text in the edited file will most likely have been 'styled' by your editor. This means that each heading, paragraph and so on has been 'tagged' to identify what type of text it is, such as a main heading, a normal text paragraph, a bulleted list or an example. This styling is used to identify text during the layout stage, but it doesn't reflect how your book will look when the layout is done – it's simply a representation of the different elements of the text of your book. (We also use colour in our text styling to help us identify what's what; I always remind authors that these colours will not be included when the book is printed.)

Once you've carefully checked the file from your editor and responded to any queries, you send the file back. Some back and forth with your editor may occur at this stage as you discuss some of the changes.

If you're not happy with anything your editor has done, don't be reluctant to raise it. It's your book and it will have your name on it. You need to be absolutely confident about everything your editor has done. Your editor will be more than happy to discuss any issues with you. He or she will be able to explain to you why any change has been made, and if you disagree on any changes, some discussion will usually be able to come up with a compromise.

Sometimes your book will go through a number of rounds of editing in Word if it needs a bit of extra work. At the outset of your project your editor or self-publishing provider should assess your manuscript and work out how many rounds of editing they think will be needed and discuss this with you.

Step 2: Editing

The second edit

The second edit will be done after the layout is complete. Your editor will go through the book one more time checking for the same issues as during the first edit and making any final corrections and refinements, and also checking the layout. This is the point where your book really starts to come together and is starting to take its final form. This stage doesn't usually involve substantial changes – it's more of a 'tidying up' phase.

You'll receive from your editor a hard copy or PDF of your completed layout to check. This is usually the second-last time you'll see your book before it's printed and your last chance to make any changes (except for any absolutely essential last-minute errors that need to be fixed at later stages).

You need to read the book very carefully at this stage. This is your chance to check it thoroughly from start to finish and pay very close attention to details. Most authors I work with usually take about a week to read and carefully check the book at this stage.

You should also be checking the layout at the same time. If a reference to a diagram on page 27 is included, go to page 27 to make sure the diagram is actually there and not on page 28. Check that any diagrams, images and tables are in the right place. Make sure all the elements of your book have been included, such as the 'about the author' or a 'further reading' list. Going back to your original manuscript and having a quick flick through to make sure nothing has been left out is a good idea.

Your editor and proofreader will be checking all of these issues for you as well, but keep in mind it's your book. It has your name on the cover. You've been working on it for months. You need to take responsibility and do your bit to make sure your book is published exactly as you want it to be. That's part of the responsibility you take on as a self-publisher.

Proofreading

Proofreading is the final step in the editing of your book. It's the final check for errors by a person who has not previously read the book. This provides a fresh set of eyes, which is essential because at this point you, your editor and your designer will have been working on the book for many weeks – or months – and will therefore be less likely to spot any problems.

Even the best of editors won't pick up every single mistake in your book, so proofreading is essential. Proofreading is Step 4 in the publishing process, so we won't go into any more detail here.

There will probably *still* be a typo or two in your book

I'm going to warn you about this now because it often upsets authors unnecessarily: despite all of the above, the odd typo or minor error may still be in your book when it comes out. Editors and proofreaders are human too, and if the above process gets rid of 99.999999 per cent of the mistakes, that still leaves a few minor errors in there.

If you go into any publishing company in Australia, you will find a corrections shelf with books marked with errors for correction when the book is reprinted. Elizabeth Flann, an icon in Australian editing and co-author of the excellent *Australian Editing Handbook*, has even admitted two mistakes appear in that book!

Finding an error in your book can be a bit disappointing, but don't let it get you down. It's really a common part of the publishing process. If you've had your book thoroughly edited and proofread, you can't do anything more. Just fix it when you reprint!

Step 2: Editing

Copyright (a publishing minefield)

Copyright is something you may have to consider during the editing process. Copyright is a minefield, and certainly something you need to be well aware of lest you blow yourself up. It's also a very commonly misunderstood area, and you can get into a lot of trouble if you use copyright material that you didn't have appropriate permission for. If you do this and get caught, you can be required to pulp your books, or in a worst-case scenario you could get sued – after you've had to pulp your books. Nobody wants that (except the lawyers), so let's have a look at some common copyright issues.

What do I need permission to reproduce?

This question is easy to answer: any material that's going in your book that isn't yours! Okay, so it's not quite that simple, but that's a good basis to start from.

How much can I reproduce of somebody else's work before I need permission?

Not even a copyright lawyer can definitively answer this question for you, and I'm certainly not a lawyer! You've probably heard figures such as it's okay to reproduce 200 words without permission, or 150 words, but this is not exactly correct. No word limits are included in copyright law.

What is central to whether copyright has been infringed is whether a 'substantial part' of a work has been used. What's a substantial part? Nobody knows! There is *no definition* of a 'substantial part' in copyright law.

So, then, how does it work? If you reproduce 200 words of a 300-word poem in your book without permission, that will be considered a 'substantial part' and you will have infringed the poet's copyright. If you reproduce 200 words of a 120,000-word book, you're probably fine. The context of the material used is important, not just the length.

What if I change a few words?

Contrary to popular belief, changing a few words here and there in material you wish to use isn't enough to avoid copyright issues. You can't copy three paragraphs from the internet and change seven words and think you're free to use the material. So, make sure your work is your own. If you didn't write it or they're not your ideas, don't use it without permission. You could get yourself in trouble, and it also won't reflect well on you or your business.

How do I 'register' my book for copyright?

You don't! Authors are often under the misapprehension that they somehow need to 'register' their book before it is protected by copyright. In many countries – such as the US and the UK – this is true, but not in Australia (which puts us in the minority). Here, the second your fingers hit the keyboard and turn your thoughts into something coherent on a page, it's protected by copyright. Hey, it's even protected if it's incoherent. You don't need to submit your manuscript anywhere or register it somehow. You have full and immediate protection from somebody infringing on your work as soon as you have written it down.

What is the 'public domain'?

'Public domain' is another term that's often misunderstood. (You'll notice a lot of misunderstanding is going on here – that's why it's a minefield!) People often take this term to mean anything that's

Step 2: Editing

available to the public, but this isn't the case. Work is only in the public domain when copyright has expired.

The laws have changed over the years so you have to be careful, but in Australia copyright generally expires 70 years after a work is published or the death of the author, whichever is later.

How do I go about obtaining permission to use somebody else's material?

It's simple: you ask them!

This is usually done via email these days. Track down the person who holds the copyright in the material you want to use and write to them outlining your request. Include such information as what your book is about, where it will be sold, how many copies will be printed, and a bit about yourself. I usually also include the relevant pages from the book, so the person can see exactly how the material will be used. (If you don't do this, the person may ask to see it anyway.) Give them as much info as you can so that they fully understand what material you want to use and how. Remember, you're asking them to help you out so make it easy for them.

It is then entirely up to the copyright holder if they want to allow you to use their material. Some people aren't at all fussed and will say yes with no hassles. Other people might request that you make changes because they're not happy with what you've done. Of course, if permission is refused you will have to remove the relevant material from your book.

The other hurdle you might face is a fee. It's not at all unreasonable for people to ask for a payment for you to use their material. They went to the time, effort and expense to prepare it. These fees can range from a few hundred dollars to a few thousand for large requests. It is your decision whether you're prepared to pay such a fee. If the material is important to your book, you would be more likely to.

The copyright holder may also have specific requests for how they wish to be acknowledged; for example, they may insist that you provide their website in the acknowledgement.

Getting the approval in writing is absolutely vital. Email is usually okay, but if you want to be extra careful or large amounts of dollars or materials are involved, get a signed hard copy agreement that states very clearly what material is going to be used and how.

Your editor or self-publishing company may be able to assist in this area. We highlight any potential areas of concern for our self-publishers, and also provide advice on how to apply for permission to reproduce material. But, we do not make the permission applications. Why? Because this is a complex legal area and it's the responsibility of the self-publisher to ensure all adequate permissions have been secured. It's not in their interests or ours to take on this responsibility. As a self-publisher I suggest you ask for advice if needed but that you make the actual applications yourself. You can get into a lot of problems if it's not done right, so even if you are using a self-publishing company, look after this side of things yourself so that you can sleep at night knowing it's been done properly.

It is customary to offer a free copy of the book to anybody whose material you use.

Isn't just an acknowledgment okay?

No! Definitely not. This is another common misconception: that you can use other people's material as long as you acknowledge where it came from. This is completely untrue. Acknowledging a source is no substitute for obtaining permission.

You may have seen a book with a note along the lines of, 'Reasonable attempts were made to contact the copyright holders of material used in this book. If you have copyright concerns about material in this book, please contact the publisher'. I've never used this and I don't think it's a good idea. It's no replacement for permission and will provide no protection whatsoever if somebody is upset about use of their material. If you're not sure, leave it out.

Will anybody even notice?

Authors sometimes think that applying for permission to use material is just alerting the copyright owner when otherwise they might never have noticed. This is quite possibly true. I've seen authors use material without permission and have no problems at all because the copyright holder was not aware of the book. It happens. But I have two major concerns about this approach:

- First and foremost, is this the way you want to do business? Using other people's material without permission just because you think you can get away with it? If you ask me, that's not cool.
- Secondly, why would you take the risk? Major copyright disputes only occur occasionally in publishing, but when they do it can be very costly and damaging to the reputation of a business.

If your permission request is knocked back, you should be glad that you asked because it means the copyright holder would not have been happy if you had used their material without permission.

Defamatory material

Another legal issue that can get you into trouble is if your book is defamatory. If your book is controversial in any way, having a lawyer go through it for you can be a very good idea.

People often think that if they're a bit vague and change a few names or details they can get around any potential defamation issues, but this is not the case. If you, for example, accuse one of your competitors of dishonest conduct without naming them but provide enough so a reader could easily figure out who it is, you can still be sued. Also keep in mind that something being true might still not be enough to protect you from defamation charges.

Lawyers

Yep – we have to go there. If you have any concerns at all about your book from a legal standpoint, get a lawyer to look at it. Your editor may highlight any potential issues, but the final responsibility for your book lies with you. If a problem arises you will get sued, not your editor. I'm more than happy to give general suggestions about these issues to self-publishers but I always conclude with a reminder that I'm not a lawyer and they should see one if they have any concerns.

ISBNs

The editing process is a good time to sort out your ISBN and a few other such issues. If you're managing your project yourself, this is something you will have to organise; if you're using a self-publishing company, they will most likely handle this for you.

ISBN stands for international standard book number. It's a unique 13-digit number that identifies not just your book but each version of your book. What do I mean by each *version*? Each different format of your book requires a different ISBN. So, if you do a hardback and a paperback, you need two different ISBNs. You also need a different ISBN for each different file format of the ebook (see Step 6 for more on file formats).

As a minimum these days three ISBNs are usually needed for a book: one for the print edition, one for the EPUB ebook and one for the Amazon ebook. (Many people will tell you that you don't need an ISBN for your Amazon ebook, which is technically correct, but I still use one. You'll read why later.)

You'll also need a new ISBN if you reprint your book and make some changes (although a few small corrections don't require a new ISBN).

Do I need an ISBN?

I'm often asked by authors if they need an ISBN. If you're selling through bricks-and-mortar bookshops or other retail outlets, or want your book to be stocked in libraries, you most definitely need an ISBN and a barcode for the print edition. Or if you want to sell your ebook on sites such as iBooks and Kobo, you need an ISBN.

If you're *not* going to sell your book through such outlets, you can get away with not having an ISBN; however, I still always suggest to my clients that they purchase one. There are two main reasons for this:

- An ISBN looks professional; remember, we're going for a high-quality book.

- If you have an ISBN, you can always change your mind and sell it through bookstores later, even if you hadn't planned to at the start. You never know what sort of reaction your book is going to get. Maybe it will be popular and you'll regret not having the option to sell it in stores. You can always add an ISBN later if and when you reprint, but you'll have to wait to do this.

Amazon ebooks and ISBNs

If you upload through the Amazon Kindle Direct system, you actually don't need an ISBN for this version of the book because Amazon will format your book for you and allocate a unique number to your book, but I prefer not to do this. I like to control as much of the process as I can, so I have the Amazon file formatted before uploading and assign this version an ISBN. This ISBN won't even actually appear on the Amazon site, but you might find other uses for this version of the book and professional publishing requires that each version of your book has an ISBN, so that's the way we manage it. If you want to have different ebook formats available for sale on your own website, for example, you should have an ISBN for each. ISBNs are not costly so it's not an area to scrimp on.

You'll find more on ebook conversion and uploading in Step 6: The ebook.

Where do I get an ISBN?

In Australia ISBNs are sold and administered by a company called Thorpe-Bowker, which provides numerous services to the bookselling and publishing industry, including magazines and newsletters, databases, sales figures, ISBNs and barcodes.

You can order ISBNs and barcodes direct from Thorpe-Bowker online, or your self-publishing expert will probably be able to provide your ISBNs and barcodes for you. This is usually the better option, for two reasons:

- It's easier. As with most things online you'll have to set up an account if you do it yourself. If you purchase it as part of your publishing pack, you don't have to worry about this. One less password to remember!

- It's usually cheaper. When you open an account with Thorpe-Bowker you have to pay a new publisher registration fee before you can purchase ISBNs. Your self-publishing provider will have done this already, so you should save a few dollars. Some services offer ISBNs for free.

If you're managing your project yourself, some ebook services offer a free ISBN with your ebook uploading; however, a couple of drawbacks are involved. Firstly, you won't know what your ISBN is until you're ready to upload your book, and I think this is too late. You want to be able to give people the ISBN for your book earlier than this, to help them order when it becomes available. You also want to have it for any publicity material you're preparing, and you'll be working on this before your book is ready for uploading. Also – and this is a very small point – when you purchase your ISBNs from one source the numbers will usually be similar and almost sequential, which I like to think is a small touch of professionalism. You'll look like a professional publisher who needs lots of ISBNs.

Make sure you buy from a reputable service provider. I've heard stories of authors being sold ISBNs that have already been allocated to other books. This will create all sorts of chaos and lost sales.

Barcodes

We all know what a barcode is and you can obtain one for your book in all sorts of ways. You can buy them from Thorpe-Bowker when you buy your ISBNs, or your designer, printer or self-publishing company might provide them.

Your barcode is generated from your ISBN and placed on the back of your book. Make sure it's not too small or covered by other material on your cover. And if you are doing it yourself, ask your designer what file format he or she would prefer.

CIP

CIP stands for Cataloguing in Publication, the very awkward name for a catalogue entry with the National Library. Having this entry isn't essential, but including it in your book is another of those little touches that separates a professionally published book from an amateur effort. A CIP entry will also help your book get picked up by libraries.

Getting an entry is free; you simply have to fill out a form on the National Library of Australia website. You need to have an ISBN to complete this form, so make sure you have organised this first.

The National Library will send you a copy of your listing via email, and this is usually included on the imprint page of the book.

Design

The cover

We've all heard the saying, 'Don't judge a book by its cover', right? Well, in the book industry we do, and you should too. The cover is the first thing you see when you walk into a bookstore or browse a website. Why would you *not* judge a book by its cover? If the cover is lousy or uninteresting, clearly the book has been poorly produced and you'll be more inclined to think that what's on the inside won't be much good either. That's not to say that if the book cover is good the book will always be good and if it's bad the book will always be bad, but after working in publishing for over 15 years I can say with great confidence that a book with a bad cover is *more likely* to not be very good. The same people who make the decisions about the cover also make the decisions about the editing, layout, printing and everything else, so if they've made a mess of the cover they're more likely to have got other stuff wrong as well. On the other hand, an attractive book inspires confidence in the quality of the work and will make you much more likely to pick up the book and have a look through.

Stand Out

One of my favourite books ever is *Life of Pi*. I happened to be in a bookshop just a few days after it came out and before all the fuss. I hadn't heard of it yet. I noticed it beside the counter. The cover was absolutely beautiful, as was the printing, and I bought it without even looking inside. Turned out to be one of the best books I ever read.

The appearance of your book matters. If the book doesn't look appealing to your target market, they're less likely to pick it up, and then it doesn't matter how good your content or your writing is, people won't read it.

Finding a designer

If you're project managing your book yourself, you will have to find a designer. As with most things these days, that's easy done on the internet. Designers have websites with portfolios on them, so these are a great place to start. Look around a number of sites and browse through a number of portfolios. Once you've found, say, three portfolios you like, get in touch with the designers and have a chat. Another way to find a good designer is to find a book cover you like – the name of the designer will be inside the book.

Discuss your business and your book and ask the designer for their thoughts and ideas. You're not just looking for a designer whose designs you like; you want to find somebody you can work with and get along with, and who understands what you are aiming for with your book. As with any service provider you're trying to find, if a designer doesn't seem too interested in chatting to you about your project or you're not happy with this initial discussion, it's time to move on to the next person on your list.

If you're using a self-publishing company to help you with your book, cover design will be part of the package. You should ask for

Step 3: Design

samples of their previous books when comparing self-publishing companies, so you can check out the kinds of covers they do.

Briefing a designer

Providing your designer or self-publishing company with a detailed brief of your cover is very important. You can't simply say: 'I want it to be blue, with a picture of a jogger on the front and the writing in yellow'. You're unlikely to get a cover you're happy with if that's all the information you provide. The designer is responsible for coming up with a good design, but you're responsible for telling them exactly what you want.

The first thing I tell people to do when discussing their cover design is to find four or five book covers (or more) that they like and that reflect how they would like their book to look. You can do this online these days on sites such as Booktopia, but it's also a good idea to go to a bookstore. You can see how the book looks on a shelf and how it stands out from other books. You can pick it up and have flick through and get a much better idea of how the book looks and feels. So I suggest you do this as a first step.

The cover of your book should align with the book's content and your business in general. If your business is accounting and your book is about payroll management, you will want it to look businesslike and perhaps a bit corporate. If your business is running parties for kids, your cover should look fun. If your book is about how to renovate a house, your cover should look practical.

When you brief your designer, include the following:
- As mentioned above, you should have found a number of book covers that reflect how you'd like your book cover to look and feel. Pass these examples on to the designer or your self-publishing company.

- Give them a synopsis of the book so they can get a feel for it. I sometimes even provide designers with a complete file of the book and ask them to have a look through it. (You can't expect them to read it from start to finish, but they can have a flick through and get a feel for the book.)
- Describe who the target market is.
- Provide any preferences you have for images, colours and fonts.
- Provide the practical details, such as the title, author name and size (format) of the book.

Your designer or self-publishing provider will usually send you four or five different design ideas to look at and discuss. At this stage, the design will no doubt need some further refining. The designer will ask you which idea is your preference, and then you can discuss that cover and make any required changes. The designer may send another two or three different ideas next time, and again you can narrow it down and refine it. You'll usually go through three or four rounds of changing and refining.

When the front cover is complete, you'll move on to the spine and back cover.

The spine and the back cover

You will, of course, also need a spine and back cover design for your book. These are usually completed after the front cover design is finalised.

Your back cover should contain:
- Blurb (sometimes also known as 'back cover copy'): don't make this too 'hard sell'. Your blurb should accurately reflect the content of your book while encouraging people to read it.

Step 3: Design

> A good way to summarise the content is using bullet points as part of the blurb.

- About the author: a few lines about you and why you're qualified to write this book.

- Barcode: this is generated from your ISBN. Your designer, printer or self-publishing service provider should be able to provide a barcode for you.

- Author photo: this is optional. If you do have an author photo, make sure it's a professional image. Don't use a photo of yourself in shorts and thongs with a beer in your hand. If you don't have any high-quality shots available, you should pay to have some done, or at least have a friend with a good camera take a photo of you in a professional outfit against a nice background.

- Web address: optional but I think it's always a good idea to include this on the back of your book.

- Price: again optional, but including the price can be a good idea because it places a value on the book. When using your book in your business, you will often give copies away for free (I gave away six books in one day last week), and having the price on the back will remind people that they have been given something of value, which will make them appreciate it more.

The spine should contain your name and the title of your book. If you have room, you can also include the subtitle of your book (if you have one). Putting your company logo on the bottom of the spine is also a good idea – this is another one of those little touches that makes your book look professional. If you don't have a company logo, you might be able to use the logo of your self-publishing company. We do this from time to time for authors who don't have a company logo they can use.

And here's a design tip for the spine of your book: make it simple, high contrast and easy to read. Too often I see books that have almost unreadable fancy lettering on the spine. What happens is the designer simply copies the elaborate typography from the front cover over to the spine and then reduces the size, but what looks good and is easy to read in 80-point type on the front often becomes unreadable in 16-point type on the spine. The lettering on the spine has to be consistent with the front cover but it doesn't have to match exactly.

If your book is in a bookstore, often people will only see the spine on a shelf with hundreds of other books. Don't make your book hard to identify with a messy spine.

Don't forget about the ebook

Designing a cover for your book these days needs to take into account that, for your ebook, the cover will be most often seen by readers as a very small image on a website. This has affected book cover design in recent years, and is something you should keep in mind.

Here are some tips for designing a cover that will work well as an ebook cover:

- Make sure the text is still legible when the cover is reduced to thumbnail size. High-contrast colours will work well.

- Use crisp, clear fonts and typography. Elaborate drop shadows, embossed-style typography and the like can make the cover harder to read when it's small.

- Don't be afraid to have a text-only cover.

Step 3: Design

- Don't use too many images.
- Don't put text over the top of a complex image.

Why you should start on your cover early

The cover design is usually done in parallel with the editing and layout of your book, but it isn't dependent on them so you can move the cover along at its own pace. So why is it helpful to get your cover as soon as you can?

Having the cover is a very useful tool for promoting your book before it comes out, so it can be very beneficial to have your cover design done as soon as you can. You can put the cover on your website, use it in social media and start preparing your publicity material. It doesn't have to be the finished version, just as long as it looks good and is close to the final design. The cover design for this book was done weeks before editing started, and we'll make a few final tweaks before the book goes to the printer.

Do books with green covers *really* not sell?

I have to mention this because I hear it from time to time: in researching book covers you may come across the old wives' tale that green books don't sell. I've never seen any evidence of this and I've never found anybody who has, and I've seen some fantastic green book covers, so if you want to use green on your cover, I say go for it!

The interior

As with the front cover of your book, a great way to find out how you want your book to look inside is to go to a bookstore and have a look through some books! Think about whether you want your book to look modern, traditional, funky, fun – whatever!

The inside of your book should match the tone of your topic. If you're an engineer, make your book look technical. If you're a financial planner, you might want to make it look a bit more serious. Also consider your target market. If you're a financial planner who targets retirees, you might want it to look serious and conservative; if you're a financial planner who works with twenty-somethings, you could make your book look serious and modern.

Book size

I could just as easily address book size (and the use of colour, following) in the printing section of this book, but this is the point that you have to make these decisions so we'll look at these two important issues now.

The size of your book (called the 'trim size' or 'format') is important. It will affect the feel and usability of your book. I recently worked on a book that was for parents of premature babies; it had photos throughout of babies and young children, and medical diagrams, so we used a larger format. But if your book is text only or predominantly text, a larger size is inappropriate. Once again, go to a bookshop or look on your shelves at home and consider book sizes. Find a book similar to yours and see what size it is. Do you think this size is appropriate? Is the content of the book appropriately sized and easy to read? How does it feel in your hands? Should it be larger, or smaller?

You will come across a number of standard trim sizes, such as 129 mm × 198 mm or 153 mm × 234 mm. Sticking to one of these sizes is a good idea because it will cost less to print and your book

Step 3: Design

won't look out of place on a shelf. (Some printers will have minor variations on the standard sizes, due to the format of their presses.) A very popular size is A5 (148 mm × 210 mm) – we often suggest this because it's a trim size just about any printer can use, and no reformatting is required for Amazon print on demand.

The trim size of your book also affects your print costs, though the difference might only be a few hundred dollars. I usually discuss the book with the author and we agree on what size is best, not what is cheapest.

Using colour inside your book

I'm often asked by authors if they can use just a few colour images here and there in their book, and the answer is you can, but you shouldn't.

It's all to do with the technicalities of printing. Books are printed in 'sections', which are page multiples of eight. To give you a rough idea, imagine a sheet of A4 paper with four book pages printed on each side, then folded and trimmed; that's an eight-page section. A 224-page book is made up of 28 eight-page sections.

If you're printing just one colour throughout your book, each of these sections will be printed black only. But if you want to add just a single colour image to one section, that whole section needs to be printed in colour, which is more expensive. If you want to spread a few colour images throughout your book, suddenly most or all of your sections need to be printed in colour, just to have, say, 10 or 15 colour images. That's hardly economical.

This is why many books requiring colour images are printed with one or two colour sections, usually in the middle of the book. Next time you're in a bookshop, have a flick through a few books in the non-fiction section, or have a look on your shelves at home. You will notice two things:

- You will not find a book that has just a few colour images scattered throughout.

- When you do find a book that has a colour section in the middle (or near the middle), the number of pages of this section will be a multiple of eight.

You may also find a book that has a section in the middle with black-and-white images on different paper. This is done because the publisher decided that the images needed higher quality paper to improve the quality of the images. They didn't want to pay for the higher quality paper throughout the book, so they just used it in a section in the middle.

If you want to use colour images, keep in mind that doing so can increase your print costs noticeably (often more than double), so you must decide if you *really* need them. If you decide that you do, you then need to decide whether to have a colour section in the middle, which will be less expensive, or to print your entire book in colour, which will be more expensive. Full-colour throughout looks great but it will increase your investment, so make sure this is money well spent for your book. For example, we recently worked on a book that contained lots of medical diagrams that were very difficult to follow without colour, so in this instance the colour printing was worth the extra investment.

It's not hard to understand that colour printing is more expensive than black only (it's not actually 'black-and-white' printing because the ink is black and the paper is white, so really only the black is printed; any single-colour printing is known as 'mono'). Full-colour printing uses four colours, though it's not four times as expensive. Many variables are involved, but colour is usually 2.5 to 3.0 times more expensive.

Can I do the layout myself?

Here's the first rule of book design and layout: don't do it yourself in Microsoft Word! Just, don't. Many self-published books have used Word, and it's obvious as soon as you open them. Word isn't a page layout program, it's a word processor. No designer or publishing professional uses Microsoft products for layout, either Word or Publisher. The results are poor compared to professional-standard programs.

Another problem with Word is that it can be an unreliable way to supply your book to the printer; in fact, some printers refuse to accept Word files or PDFs created in Word. Things can move around and fonts can be replaced without the printer realising. Colour can be difficult to control, and margins can shift without your knowledge. In PDFs created in Word, sometimes fonts don't function properly. I've had numerous requests from printers to perform rescue jobs on files that have been supplied to them in Word. It's not pretty.

So, don't do it yourself in Word (or Publisher). It will look like rubbish and your printer will not be happy.

If you can't use Microsoft anything, what can you use? This is easy: a book layout professional. You're trying to produce a professional-quality book, right? So don't do it yourself – and don't have it done by somebody who has never laid out a book before either. I worked with a self-publisher a few years ago who had given the book to her photographer for layout because he used a page layout program to prepare photo displays and thought he could handle a book. I told her this was a bad idea, but after I gave her the edited files I didn't hear from her again. I did, however, receive a call from the printer when they received the files that had been formatted by the photographer. He had started page 1 of the book on the left-hand page, a publishing stuff-up and obvious sign of an amateur book. (Have a look at the books on your shelves – the odd-numbered pages will *always* be on the right side.) The printer – quite reasonably – refused to print the book because it could easily be assumed that the printer had messed it up, not the designer. They asked me to rescue the project. Needless to say, it cost a lot of time and money to fix.

You may have somebody at work who 'does your newsletter' or a cousin who likes to 'play around in Photoshop', but if you have them lay out your book the results are likely to leave you wishing you'd spent the money to do it properly. I could fill a whole chapter just with stories where authors have tried to save money and time only to expend more of both when we've had to come in and salvage a book that has turned to porridge. Doing it yourself or using an inexperienced person means more time, money and hassle, not less.

As with printing and many other things to do with books, always use an experienced professional. And that means experienced with books, not newsletters, websites, brochures, logos, Photoshop or designing business cards. Books.

Proofreading and indexing

Proofreading

Proofreading is the final quality-control step in the production of your book. Even the best of editors won't pick up every single problem and error in your book, so proofreading is essential. It will be the difference between a professional-standard book and one that's not quite there. One or two minor errors in your book aren't the end of the world, but if you don't have it proofread there will be much more than that, and this will reflect poorly on you and your business, which completely undermines everything you're trying to achieve by publishing a book. I sometimes hear people say that a book they read was full of mistakes and it wasn't edited; it's much more likely that it was edited but it wasn't proofread.

You may think that it's been read numerous times during the editing stage and so surely there can't be any mistakes left, right? Wrong. By the end of the editing process you're the last person who will find any mistakes in your book. You may have spent three months or six months writing it, and another month or two – or three – on the editing, layout and cover. By this point you (and your editor) will be so close to your book that some of the pages could be upside down and you might not notice. You need fresh eyes.

Editors and proofreaders can have particular things they like to change and other things they are happy to let go. (Editing can be as much art as science.) Something that one editor might not even register may be something that another always addresses, so combining an editor with a different proofreader means you cover more bases. Also, a proofreader reads the book in a different way, really focusing on line by line, word by word and letter by letter, not really concerning themselves with more 'editorial' areas. The proofreader will assume that the author and editor are happy with the content – their role is just to look for mistakes, nothing more.

If you're managing your project yourself, you need to find a proofreader and coordinate the process with your editor. Your proofreader will provide changes on hard copy (or maybe in a marked up PDF); it's a good idea to pass these changes on to your editor and ask them to have a look at them. Once your editor has marked which changes are to be taken in and which can be ignored (some of them will just be suggested changes), the proofread copy of the book will be passed on to your designer to take in the final corrections. Or, you may be able to ask your editor to handle this whole step for you.

If you're using a self-publishing provider, proofreading will be included, and it's a step in the process you may not even be involved in. Authors I work with know when their book is being proofread, but we only involve them in the process if the proofreader raises an issue that needs their attention, which very rarely happens.

Keep in mind that the only person qualified to proofread your book is an experienced editor or proofreader. Your next-door

Step 4: Proofreading and indexing

neighbour might be a retired English teacher but that doesn't necessarily make them a proofreader.

Indexing

An index is a valuable tool to help readers find what they want in your book, though I have noticed fewer and fewer authors are including an index in recent times. An index goes at the very back of your book, and lists all the major topics in your book in considerable detail.

Authors sometimes confuse an index with the contents page at the front of the book. The contents page lists the titles of the chapters and the page numbers, and sometimes the major headings in each chapter as well. The index goes at the back of the book and lists the major subjects covered and the relevant page numbers. It goes into much more detail than the contents list: a comprehensive index could have 500 entries while the contents page of the same book might have 15 entries.

Your editor may also be able to do your index, and this can be a good option. Being more familiar with a book can result in a more nuanced and effective index. This is because creating an index is much more involved than simply listing every instance of a word or subject that appears in the book. An indexer will carefully assess the major topics in your book and only index those topics and mentions of that topic that are of benefit to the reader. If a topic is only mentioned in passing on a certain page, it won't be included in the index.

If your editor doesn't also do indexing, you'll have to find an indexer. This is easy done with an internet search. Or, if you're using a self-publishing service provider they will be able to take care of the index for you.

Indexes and ebooks

Unfortunately the index created for your print book can't be used as is for your ebook, because, as explained elsewhere, an ebook doesn't have 'pages' as such so an index with page numbers isn't much help. 'Page 70' on your tablet will be different from 'page 70' on your smartphone – if there is a page 70 at all, depending on the software being used to read the book.

You can have the print index re-formatted for your ebook. Creating an index for an ebook is a bit involved; it's done with hyperlinks, like a web page, so when you click on the link in the index you're taken to the relevant page. An index is optional for an ebook because ebooks are searchable, so it's actually not too hard for readers to find what they're looking for.

Printing

Ten or fifteen years ago it was very easy to recognise a self-published book. The design was poor, you didn't have to look too hard to find errors or other unprofessional touches such as no ISBN or barcode, and numerous other clues. But often the biggest giveaway was obvious before you even opened the book: the quality of the printing was poor. The paper was cheap, the binding was loose and the cover lamination peeled off after a few weeks. If you sneezed while holding it, the whole book would fall apart. Because self-publishers often print lower quantities, this lower standard of printing was all they had access to.

Fortunately, that has changed dramatically in the last few years.

Why print quality is so important

High-quality printing is absolutely pivotal to producing a professional book. Great content, beautiful design and outstanding editing will all be undone with poor-quality printing. A book that doesn't feel nice when it's picked up, is difficult to open and has poor reproduction is not a good reflection on your business, no matter how well everything else has been done. But with the huge advances in printing technology in recent years, high-quality book printing is now available to everybody. Because this is vital to the success of your book, in this step we're going to examine the issues in detail so you can make a well-informed choice about the printing of your book.

Printing options

If you're project managing your book yourself, knowing the different printing methods available to you is helpful. If you're using a self-publishing company, you probably won't be as involved in the finer details of the print management, but the following information will still help you understand what is happening with your book.

High-quality printing has always been available for larger print runs, but because most self-publishers only print a few hundred copies this high-quality printing was usually beyond reach for them. The reason is that basically two different printing methods are available: one that is more economical for higher print quantities and one for lower quantities. Up until recently, the method for printing lower quantities (often called 'short-run printing') was noticeably poorer in quality.

Offset printing

I won't go into great deal about the technicalities, but you might come across the term 'offset printing' in your self-publishing journey. The only technical thing you really need to know about offset printing is it's the method used for printing larger print runs.

Step 5: Printing

Offset printing is an industrial endeavour. You've probably seen those huge presses in the movies, usually printing newspapers. That's what offset printing is like. Webs of paper travel through the large presses (known as 'web presses'). First the pages are printed, then folded and trimmed, and then bound and attached to the cover on a binder. It's a large, interesting, impressive process.

Because it operates on such a large scale, offset printing is only economical for larger print runs. There is no fixed quantity at which offset printing becomes viable because it depends on the specifications of the individual book, such as trim size and page extent – it generally becomes economically viable for quantities around 700 to 1000 and above.

Digital printing

Like so many industries in recent years, publishing has been transformed by the digital revolution. Ebooks, on-screen editing, desktop publishing – all have been transformative. But no area of publishing has benefited from new technology more than printing.

Unlike an offset printing press, a digital printer is not a large, industrial-scale machine. My printer recently installed a whole new digital book printing system which does binding, trimming and everything in one, and it looks like a very, very large photocopier. Load up a PDF, press print, and a book comes out the other end!

Digital printing has in fact been around for years, but until recently the quality wasn't great. Five or six years ago I could easily tell a digitally printed book from an offset book from three metres away. The tones in the images were uneven, the image resolution was poor, the paper was low quality, the cover was dull. I have a few books on my shelf from a number of years ago for which I have a digitally printed edition and an offset version, and the differences are stark.

One of the biggest issues was the binding. We've all had the experience of a book that seems to be bound 'tightly'. You feel like it's trying to snap shut all the time – it's actually an effort to hold it open. Get distracted for a second and the book shuts and you lose your place. As a reader it's one of my pet hates that really interferes with my reading enjoyment. A book should encourage you to read it, not fight you. This is one of the key things I look for in a printer. Digital printing used to have real problems getting this right. Not any more. These days telling the difference between digitally and offset printed books is much more difficult.

Along with these improvements, with the advances in technology and growth in popularity short-run prices have come down dramatically.

This improvement in print quality and affordability is one of the key drivers of the huge growth in self-publishing in recent years (along with ebooks). It's possible to print 100 copies of a book that you can be proud of, rather than it looking like a poor substitute for a 'properly published' book.

Print on demand

You have probably heard of print on demand, known in the industry simply as 'POD'. This is the extreme end of digital printing, allowing you to have single copies of your book printed, to a quality you will be more than happy with. Through companies such as Lightning Source (which has a plant and office in Melbourne), you can have your book available in bookshops (if you use the right distributor) and to order on sites such as Amazon without ever printing a single

Step 5: Printing

copy in advance. The book is printed only when it's ordered by a bookstore or on a website. The printer will print, bind and mail out the book within a few days of the order. The customer will have no idea the book was only printed when they ordered it.

If you set up with a print on demand service, you can print one copy, 100, 500, or as many as you need. You can order books yourself and have them delivered to your door. A number of small publishers use this exclusively as their printing and distribution method.

So, which one is right for me?

Each method has advantages and disadvantages, and I use all three methods all the time. Deciding which method to use is based on what the goals and requirements are for each project.

One author I've worked with for years planned from day one to print only 200 copies of his book, and to reprint whenever his stock got low. He has now self-published four books, and I hear from him a few times a year with an order for another 200 copies of one of his books. We print his books digitally.

Another author I worked with recently wanted 2500 copies, of which he was going to give away 2000 copies to existing and potential clients. That's done with offset printing.

Another author I spoke to recently wanted to test the waters with her first book before committing to a larger print run, so initially she's using print on demand.

For quantities around 700 to 1000 copies, deciding whether offset or digital is preferable can be difficult. Some printers have both methods, so you can simply ask them which is more economical for your requirements. If you can't find a printer that does both, approach both an offset and a digital printer and ask for quotes. If you're managing your printing yourself, you need to understand which method will be more economical for you, otherwise you could end up paying hundreds – or even thousands – of dollars more for your printing.

If you're using a self-publishing professional, this is probably not something you'll need to worry about; your expert will handle all of this for you. We don't usually discuss digital versus offset with our self-publishers. They simply leave it to us and trust us to make the right decisions for their printing.

There is only one exception to this: while I've said repeatedly that the quality of digital printing has improved greatly, at the high end of the scale offset printing is still better quality. For 99 per cent of projects the quality of digital is fine, but if print quality is vital to the success of your book – for example, if you're a high-end photographer, or an interior designer and colour is pivotal – offset printing will give you the best results. Despite the advances in digital, the image resolution is just that little bit better with offset printing, as is the quality of the colour, and higher quality papers are also usually available. So, if you're producing a high-end book where colour is crucial, you may have to use offset printing to get the results you desire, even though it may cost more.

Choosing a printer

So, how do you find the right printer for you? Two of the major book printers in Australia are Griffin Press (based in Adelaide) and McPherson's Printing (based in Maryborough in regional Victoria, with offices in Melbourne). There are also many smaller book

Step 5: Printing

printers, and many general print shops these days also offer book printing. Both McPherson's and Griffin are used by Australia's major publishers, and they will also work with self-publishers.

Once you've found a few printers you'd like to investigate, give them a call and discuss your project to see if they can help. The two most important things you need to find out about are the quality of their book printing and their costs. Both of these are easy to do.

To find out about the quality of their printing, simply ask them to send you a sample copy of a book they have recently printed. Any quality printer will do this without hesitation. If the printer is reluctant to do so, they've made your decision easy; don't use them. Make sure they send you a *book* they've printed, not a brochure, poster or anything else. I've seen printers who will print a book because their machines can do it but they have no particular interest or skill in this area and the results are commensurate with the attitude.

When the printer sends you a sample copy, have a close look at it and answer the following questions:

- Do the images look sharp?
- Is the printing even in tone?
- Is the binding solid and the book easy to open?
- Is the paper good quality?
- Is the lamination smooth and even?
- Does the book feel high quality, or does it feel flimsy and cheap?

Once you have satisfied yourself that the printer can meet your quality needs, it's time to get a quote.

You'll need to give the printer the following information:

- How many copies you want printed. Get quotes on a number of quantities, such as 200, 300 and 500, so you can see what your options are.

- The size of your book (known in publishing as the 'trim size').

- The length of your book (called the 'page extent').

- Whether it has any colour inside.

- Where you need copies delivered to.

- How you will be supplying files – usually this is PDF files.

- What type of binding you want.

- What type of lamination you want.

- What type of paper you want for the text and cover (known as the 'stock').

Don't hesitate to use a printer or your self-publishing professional as a source of advice. Any good printer or self-publishing provider will spend some time with you answering these questions. Good, reliable service is also important. If you're not satisfied with the quality of service, find somebody else. There are plenty of good printers out there – don't waste your time with a dodgy one.

If you hire a self-publishing professional they will handle all of this for you, but it's still useful for you to know what's going on. As with selecting a printer, when you're searching for a self-publishing service provider have them send you sample copies of books they have printed recently. Take note of the print quality and use this as a factor in your decision of which provider to use. If you're not sure what your print requirements are, that's even more of a reason to discuss printing with your potential suppliers!

Step 5: Printing

If you're managing the project yourself, your designer and printer may need to liaise during your project to confirm specifications for your book. Any professional printer and designer will be happy to do this for you.

Unit cost

'Unit cost' is the print cost per book. Here is the golden rule of working out unit cost: calculate it on how many books you *sell* (or use), not how many you *print*.

Self-publishers often notice the lower unit cost that comes with printing higher quantities and decide they should print more. This is never a good idea if you're doing so just to get the lower unit cost. Your print run should always be based on how many copies of the book you need, not on the unit cost. If you work out a plan for your book that suggests you need 300 copies but then print 500 to get the cheaper unit cost, how does that help you if it turns out your plan was spot on and you have 200 copies left in your garage? Remember, you can always reprint very quickly.

Work out a plan for how many copies you think you need, with careful research, reasoning and explanations. How many do you think you can sell? How many will you use for publicity? How many will you give away to potential clients? How else might you use them? Now, working out print quantities isn't an exact science. If publishers could work out down to the last copy how many books we needed to print, we'd all be millionaires. But it is possible to make an informed decision based on how you're going to use the book in your business; this is what your print run should be based on, not the unit cost.

It's also important to think of this from a cash flow point of view. If you think you can sell 1000 copies over 12 months, printing 500 copies initially and the next 500 copies six months later will be a lot better for your cash flow. Your unit cost will be slightly higher than printing 1000 but your cash flow will be better. With modern printing technology the difference in unit costs over shorter runs has come down so this is not as much of an issue as it was, say, 10 years ago.

Also keep in mind that if you're printing a larger run, due to the vagaries of the printing process you won't usually receive *exactly* the number of books you ordered. If you're printing 3000 copies, you may actually receive 2977 copies, or 3015, and you will be charged accordingly. The allowable variation specified by most printers is plus or minus 5 per cent. If you're not happy with this, talk to your printer. You may be able to order on an 'exact quantity' basis, which means your printer will deliver the exact quantity specified. Not all printers will do this. This is generally only relevant for offset printing. This is not usually something you have to worry about with smaller, digital print runs.

Spine width

Once you get towards the end of the interior layout of your book, you need to find out from your printer how wide the spine of your book will be. This is dependent on a number of issues:

- the page extent of your book
- the thickness of the paper you're using
- the binding method of your book
- whether your book is hardback or paperback.

Step 5: Printing

Once you've finalised the page extent of your book, simply contact your printer and ask them for the spine width. This can then be passed on to your cover designer so that he or she can finalise your cover. If you're using a self-publishing company, you won't need to worry about this – it will be done for you.

Paper

You need to think about a number of things when choosing the paper (stock) for your book:

- Colour: non-fiction books are usually printed on whiter stock, whereas fiction books are more often printed on a creamy-coloured stock.

- Quality: if you have images in your book you might select slightly better paper to improve the quality of the image reproduction. You can use the higher quality paper throughout the book, or you can have an image section in the middle of your book (colour or black and white) printed on the better stock, and the text sections of your book printed on slightly lower quality stock.

- Weight: most stock for books is around 80 GSM for the text (the 'internals') and 250 to 300 GSM for the cover.

- Bulk: the weight of the stock doesn't necessarily reflect its thickness. Some stocks are bulkier (that is, thicker) than others. The primary reason for using a bulkier stock is if your book is short and you want it to appear more substantial.

Discuss these issues with your self-publishing service provider or your printer. Any good printer will be able to provide you with paper samples. Explain to them what you need and take their advice. Also keep in mind that varying the paper can affect the print costs for your book, sometimes significantly.

Lamination

The two basic choices for cover lamination are gloss and matt. (It's often thought that matt covers are actually not laminated, but this is incorrect. They're laminated with a matt finish.)

Gloss lamination is the most common. It makes the colours on a cover look brighter, and is also more resistant to marking and scratching. However, matt looks great on the right cover. Talk this over with your designer and/or your printer and decide what is best for your book.

Another option is UV coating, which has a semi-gloss look and is usually cheaper than gloss lamination. Different printers and self-publishing providers will offer different options.

Proofs

You will receive proofs of the text and cover of your book from the printer, usually PDFs via email these days.

Keep in mind that this is not a chance to make editorial corrections; you're simply checking that the printer has reproduced your files correctly. You *can* make changes at this stage if you really must, but it will cost you and also hold up your printing. As such you should only make corrections if you find a major error.

If you're using a self-publishing company, you probably won't see the printer's proofs. I don't usually show the printer's proofs to our self-publishers; they are paying me to make sure their book

Step 5: Printing

prints correctly so it's my responsibility to make sure the proofs are right.

If your book contains colour inside and this is vital to the book, you might like to request hard-copy proofs. These will most likely cost extra (perhaps a few hundred dollars), but they will give you a more accurate reproduction than a PDF and allow you to carefully check the accuracy of the colour.

Advance copies

When your book is printed, the printer will usually send a couple of copies to you for inspection before delivering the stock. These copies are known as 'advance copies' or simply 'advances'.

This is your chance to inspect the books and approve them for delivery. Things to look out for include:

- The general quality of the printing; is it even and are the colours accurate?
- Margins: is the text placed correctly on the page?
- The binding: does the book feel sturdy, with no pages falling out?
- Everything in the right place: everybody in publishing has seen this at one time or another – pages of a book inserted upside down. It's rare but it happens! Also make sure the pages are sequential. It is possible for sections to be bound out of order.
- Lamination: is it well attached to the cover and not peeling off?

If, after you've carefully inspected the advance copies, you're happy with them, you can contact the printer and ask them to deliver the bulk stock. If you find a problem, you can call the printer to discuss the issue. If it's a small problem, such as minor variations in colour, you may be able to negotiate a discount on the printing and still use the books. If the problem is major, such as pages missing or upside down, the printer will have to reprint the books at their expense, and the faulty copies will most likely be pulped and the paper recycled. Errors that are your fault – such as layout mistakes – are not a reason to reject advances.

It is extremely rare that advance copies are rejected. In over 15 years of publishing I've done it only three or four times, and I've managed the printing of many hundreds of books in that time. (One of the times I had to reject advances was the first book I ever worked on! When the advances arrived random ink smudges appeared throughout the books. Inspection of the bulk stock revealed the same problem. This was entirely the printer's fault and nothing to do with me, but with my grand total of about two months' experience in publishing I was convinced I'd done something wrong and would be looking for a new job very soon.)

If you're printing offshore, having advance copies sent can be a good way to get a few boxes of your book sent quickly. Offshore printing takes two or three months and the bulk stock of books is sent by sea. (If you sent the bulk stock by air, you would basically undo the savings you had made by printing offshore.) But, if you need books urgently, you can have a few boxes sent over by air with your advances, so that you have say, 200, copies of your book a few weeks ahead of the bulk stock arriving. This can be very advantageous because you can start sending out publicity copies before the bulk stock arrives, which means you can get publicity for you book sooner. (See Part II for more on sending out publicity copies of your book.)

Step 5: Printing

If you're printing a really small run – say, 50 copies – the printer often won't send advances. They will simply send the 50 copies at once.

As with most things in this book, if you're using a publishing professional to help with your book this person should be happy to check the advances for you. I always check the advances for our clients – as with the proofs, they're paying me to make sure everything in this area is taken care of.

Delivery

There's a few things you'll need to clarify with your printer to make sure you aren't surprised later by extra delivery costs:

- If you are printing a large quantity – say, 3000 copies – the delivery in your quote may be based on unloading at a warehouse with a forklift. If you don't have a forklift – as most self-publishers don't! – you need to tell your printer. You'll need to request what is usually called 'trolley unload' or 'hand unload'.

- If you are sending books to more than one location – for example, copies to you and to a distributor – you need to let your printer know so it's included in your quote.

- If you don't live in the city where the printer is located, make sure the quote includes delivery to your location.

- If you are printing offshore, your quote will often include delivery only into port, not to your door. Most printers can arrange delivery to your door for an extra cost, or you can manage it yourself. Doing it yourself will probably be cheaper but also more of a hassle. I always ask my offshore printer to deliver direct to my door or to my distributor, whatever is required. (As is usually the case, anything you save in dollars is lost in extra time and hassles if you do it yourself.)

If you are using a self-publishing professional, this person will manage all these issues for you.

Reprints

If you are at the point of thinking about reprinting your book – congratulations! It's every publishers' dream to have to reprint a book.

With offset printing reprints can be about 5 to 15 per cent cheaper than the first printing. This is because the plates for the book have already been made, and they are kept by the printer. This also means reprints are quicker, usually by about 3 to 5 days in Australia and perhaps a few weeks offshore.

With digital printing, reprints may not actually be any cheaper than the first printing. This is because there are no plates in digital printing, so there's no saving from having printed the book previously.

Reprint corrections

As mentioned earlier, if you go into any publishing house in Australia they will have a shelf or file of reprint corrections, to be made if and when a book is reprinted. Despite everybody's best efforts, books are unfortunately still published with mistakes in them, usually small typos or minor formatting errors. Reprints are your chance to correct these.

Step 5: Printing

Your designer or self-publishing professional will be able to make these changes for you, and you can just supply PDFs of the relevant pages to the printer. There's no need to re-supply material for the whole book (unless you are changing a large number of pages).

Keep in mind that if you are making significant changes – for example, 20 pages – your printer may consider this a new job and not a reprint. If you think this might be an issue, call your printer to find out how many pages you can change before they consider it a new project, and then see if all the changes you are making are absolutely essential.

The ebook

As with music, movies, photography, television and many other industries in recent years, publishing has been turned on its head by the digital revolution and the invention and proliferation of ebooks.

Ebooks have some huge advantages. As a reader, it's great being able to download a book at 10 o'clock at night without getting off the couch, and they are cheaper than print books. For publishers (and especially small publishers) ebooks solve two significant problems: distribution and printing. With ebooks a small publisher can have the same distribution reach as Penguin. You can sell all over the world. And print costs are a major outlay that suddenly disappears with ebooks (although there are other formatting costs instead).

But ebooks have two major drawbacks for publishers: because of the low price expectations of readers the profit margins on ebooks are lower, and the formatting of ebooks is a bit limited compared to print.

Ebook file formats

A number of different file formats are used for ebooks. The most common is EPUB, and you'll need a MOBI file for Amazon.

EPUB

EPUB is the most common ebook format used by the vast majority of ebooks stores and readers. EPUB – not surprisingly – stands for electronic publication.

Like websites, ebooks have to be readable on a variety of different screens, such as mobile phones, tablets and laptops. For this reason, ebook text is what is known as 'reflowable'. This means that the 'page size' adjusts to whatever size the screen is and the text 'reflows' to fit this page size. For this reason, ebooks don't actually have fixed pages. On your mobile phone an ebook might be 600 'pages' long but on your tablet the same ebook might be only 300 'pages' long. To get around this problem, ebooks have what are known as 'locations'; each 'location' is attached to a section of text and moves with the text when it moves.

Unfortunately, the need for reflowable text means that ebook formatting can be rather limited. When designing a layout for printing, your design and text layout can be adjusted down to the millimetre (or down to the pixel, really) and you know this is exactly how the book will look when printed. But because in ebooks the text needs to move and the file needs to work on a range of devices, precise layouts are very difficult. So you need to be prepared for the fact that your ebook may not look as good as your print version.

Another issue is that, unfortunately, EPUB files can be a bit buggy, and you may experience minor layout errors. The EPUB format is improving but at the time of writing it seems almost impossible to entirely remove minor formatting issues, especially if your book contains a range of different text styles, lists or tables. I'm yet to read an ebook that didn't have at least some minor layout gremlins, such as inconsistent font sizes or text not lining up exactly as it should.

Step 6: The ebook

If your book is predominantly text, these errors should be minor; if you have lots of tables, diagrams or images in your book, be aware that your ebook layout might be a little underwhelming when compared to the print book.

Ebooks are still in their infancy, and the current EPUB format is – from a technical point of view – really just a packaged up website, so it still has a long way to go. And making ebooks readable on a variety of different screens and devices will always be a challenge. However, with technology in this area advancing every day I'm sure things will improve in the next few years.

MOBI

MOBI is the ebook format used exclusively by Amazon, for no other apparent reason than to lock customers into buying from Amazon when they have an Amazon device. The book will look slightly different, but it's basically the same as EPUB. However, it can only be used with an Amazon device or software.

Most ebook conversion services will supply you with an EPUB file and a MOBI file as part of their standard service. If you only have an EPUB or a MOBI file, you can download free software that will convert to other formats for you.

Other formats

Technically any file format you can put your book into can be an ebook, such as a Word file or PDF. You're unlikely to use a Word file as this would offer no protection against changes to the file, but PDFs with appropriate security can be useful. For example, you can use them on your website to provide a free sample chapter, or even your whole book.

The major advantage of PDF files is that, unlike EPUBs and MOBI, the text doesn't reflow so you can make the layout more precise, as with print. But this is also the major disadvantage of PDF files – the text doesn't reflow so your book will be difficult to read on some screens, such as a smartphone.

The formats you're most likely to use are EPUBs to list on most of the bookstores, MOBI to sell your book on Amazon and perhaps PDF to put a sample chapter on your website.

Ebook pricing

Ebook pricing is a tricky issue. Unfortunately, the wave of ebooks priced from 99¢ to $2.99 has led to many readers not expecting to pay too much for ebooks. The reasoning seems to be that because the publisher didn't have to pay for printing, the ebook should be much cheaper than the print version. But should it really be that cheap? Of course not. Printing only accounts for a small percentage of the price of a book, so the fact that ebooks don't need printing doesn't mean they should be $2.99. What you're predominantly paying for in a book is the information that it contains. You're paying for the skill and knowledge of the author, and the skills of the publisher in putting the book together. And in an ebook you're still getting these.

But arguing about the logic (or lack thereof) in ebook pricing is pointless. The fact is that people expect them to cost significantly less than the print book, and you'll just have to accept this. If you want to be stubborn and charge the same price for your ebook as your print book, you're most welcome to, but you'll be rewarded with very few sales.

Step 6: The ebook

As with pricing anything, the best place to start is to see what similar products are selling for. This will give you an excellent guide as to what the market will pay. And if you notice the sale price for similar ebooks seems to be increasing, you can price your ebook accordingly.

Significant research has been done on ebook pricing and how it affects sales, and going over $10 seems to see sales drop markedly. So, on this basis, you should have a good reason to go over $10 for your ebook. If your book is highly specialised or you're aiming for a higher end market, over $10 might be fine.

A great advantage of ebooks is it's very easy to change the price. You simply log into your account (or ask your self-publishing expert to do it for you) and change it! This means you can experiment with pricing and see what level generates the most profit for you. Is it better to sell fewer copies at a higher price or more copies at a cheaper price? Just don't adjust the price too often, or you'll annoy lots of readers.

Does my ebook need an index?

The index that you may have done for your book has to be substantially reformatted if it's going to be used in your ebook. With ebooks being searchable it's worth asking if this is worth doing.

I always tell my authors that an index is optional for the ebook and that it will cost extra. When I explain to them that ebooks are searchable and this largely eliminates the need for an index, they usually decide to go without. (Although, as mentioned earlier, more authors seem to be skipping the index for print books as well these days.)

Ebook stores

The number of ebook stores has grown rapidly in recent years, as you'd expect. Some volatility has also occurred, with takeovers, mergers and collapses.

You can manage your ebook distribution in two basic ways: like many things, you can do it yourself or have somebody manage it for you.

DIY ebook distribution

Some things in your book publishing journey can provide wildly different results if you try to do them yourself versus paying a professional; ebook distribution is *not* one of those. All you need to do to manage your ebooks yourself is a bit of time and some reasonable computer skills.

If you're going to do it yourself, you can set up accounts on each individual ebook store you wish to sell on and upload your files yourself. Setting up the accounts can be a bit fiddly but isn't difficult. You provide the information you'd expect, such as price, an author bio and ISBN, and then upload your files.

Keep in mind one major drawback of doing it all yourself is that for some US-based sites you will need a US tax ID to receive your payments. What's required to get a US tax ID? I have absolutely no idea; every time I've explained this to an author they've decided that it all sounds like a bit of a hassle and asked me to handle their ebook distribution for them, and the service we use doesn't require a US tax ID.

The other DIY option is to use what's known as an 'ebook aggregator'. This is where you upload to just one site and they upload your book to a large range of ebook stores – for a fee, of course!

Step 6: The ebook

Many ebook aggregators are available, so if this interests you just do an internet search and check out the options. Some of them will charge you a set-up fee, and then there will usually be either an ongoing annual fee or a commission on sales.

One advantage of using an ebook aggregator is that with some of them you can get around the need for a US tax ID, often by arranging payment through Paypal.

Many ebook aggregators are US-based, and as such they don't upload your ebook to Australian ebook stores, so you may have to do this yourself.

The upload

If you're uploading your ebook yourself, you will usually need the following information and files handy:

- The ebook file in EPUB format.
- The cover file in JPG format (you may need to save several different versions if you're uploading to multiple sites because they have differing requirements).
- A brief author bio.
- A description of your book.
- The keywords people would use to search for your book.
- The price (often in US dollars).
- The ISBN.
- Information required for payment, such as your bank account details or Paypal information.
- Which countries you wish to sell in (for some sites) – for most people this will simply be worldwide.

Paying others to do your ebook distribution

You can pay to have the whole ebook distribution taken off your hands. Many self-publishing service providers will handle this for you these days, as will some bookshop distributors. Which option you choose will depend on your priorities. The more you do yourself the more money you will save but the more time and energy you'll have to put in.

What is digital rights management and why should I care?

You may never have heard of digital rights management (often known as DRM), but you will be familiar with the concept. Ebooks are subject to copyright concerns in ways that printed books are not: like any computer file, an ebook can simply be copied! This is an issue that has also troubled the music, television, photography and movie industries and, after initially dealing with the whole thing very badly, these industries eventually learned to manage it. Unfortunately, it seems the publishing industry is determined to go down the difficult and ineffective path first before coming to grips with the new world of ebooks, just like music, movies and television before it.

As with these other industries, publishing has gone for the seemingly obvious solution of placing copy protection on ebook files when they are sold – this is 'digital rights management'. The idea is simple: when ebook files are sold – not when they're created; the DRM is applied by the retailer – they are encoded so that they can only be used by the person who purchased them and can't be copied. So how well do you think that's worked? Just like movies and music, it hasn't. For example, author John Birmingham

Step 6: The ebook

recently wrote a blog about how all of his ebooks had been released with DRM, and *within hours* of release they were all available on the internet for illegal download. How does this happen? Computer hackers out there are just as smart as the people inside the publishing companies and ebook retailers, and whatever solutions the publishers and retailers come up with these hackers will be able to overcome. The only way to make a computer file completely safe is to make it *impossible* to copy, but this is no use because the legitimate buyer needs to be able to download the ebook. Basically publishers have not been able to come up with a solution that will allow their legitimate customers to download ebooks but then not allow anybody else to pirate them.

The downside of DRM for readers is it makes it less convenient for them to purchase and read ebooks. DRM locks readers into a single platform; on your Kindle you can only download ebooks from Amazon, on a Kobo ebook reader you can only download ebooks from Kobo. Understanding why ebook retailers want to lock their customers in isn't hard, but it comes at the expense of ease and convenience for readers. It also means you can't freely move the book around on your different devices – and this is a book you've legitimately paid for. Some people argue that DRM actually encourages piracy because people want to be able to use their ebooks how they like, not how the retailers say they should.

So, what should you do? Well, sometimes you won't have a choice, because many of the ebook retailers you sell through will simply apply DRM automatically whether you want to or not. But, when you have a choice, it's up to you. Most authors still choose to have DRM. It seems to be a reflex; they think *some* protection must be better than none. But, really, it's not. This is how the internet is always going to work. DRM inhibits people who want to purchase your book legitimately but does nothing to stop the pirates. Doesn't sound that great does it?

Can I do an ebook only?

You can do an ebook only, but when self-publishing for your business it's not a great idea. Here's why: let's say you're in a meeting with a potential client and you mention that you've written a book. The potential client says, 'Hey, that's great. Where can I get a copy?'

You can respond to this in two ways:

> **Option A:** 'It's available on my website. When you get back to the office, go to www.mybusiness.com.au, click on the book page, and then download the EPUB file. Then, you can read it on your computer, or you can copy it to your tablet or smartphone using Dropbox or similar software, and open it in an ebook app, except if you have a Kindle. If you don't have ebook reader software, simply do an internet search, download and install the software, and then you'll be able to read it.'

> **Option B:** 'I have one in my suitcase. Here it is.'

Which response do you think is more likely to get your book read?

There's nothing like being able to hand over a printed book to somebody on the spot, rather than expecting them to download it later. Australia's number one small business author Andrew Griffiths calls this 'thud value', and it is very valuable indeed. Successful business authors *always* have a box of their books in the boot of their car and give them away at any opportunity. You simply can't do this with an ebook.

Distribution

Launching your book

A common question from authors is: 'What do I do for a book launch?' The answer is simple: you do anything you want! My father was a writer so I've been around books my whole life, and I've seen it all when it comes to launches. When I was kid we had a book launch in our lounge room. I've been to intimate book launches in restaurants and launches with 400 people in conference centres. I've been to book launches at bookshops, libraries, art galleries, hotels, pubs – you get the idea.

Your book launch does a number of things. It's a chance for you to celebrate with family and friends, it marks the publication of your book, and it's an opportunity to publicise and sell your books.

Celebrating

This is one of the main reasons you have a book launch – because it's fun! Make sure you put the business side of things away at least for a little while, and enjoy the event. It's a great achievement to have written a book, and publishing it yourself is even more impressive.

Stand Out

So invite your friends and family and pop a bottle of your favourite champagne. You've earned it.

Mark the publication of your book

First-time authors often ask me what it means to 'launch' a book. There are really no rules. Usually you'll have a guest say a few words about how awesome you are and how hard you've worked on the book, and then you can say a few words. Although they're called 'launches' there is really no official way to 'launch' a book – although I did hear about an author recently who took it literally and fired a copy of his book 100 metres into the air.

Publicity and sales

As well as being a celebration, a launch is a great way to generate interest in your book. You can send out a media release promoting your launch. You can even turn it into an event: if you've written a cook book, do a cooking demonstration. If you've written a book about architecture, hold the launch in a heritage building and give people a tour.

Celebrities can be another great hook. If you don't know any celebrities, nothing is stopping you contacting one to see if they're interested – just send them a copy of your book and tell them about the launch. Your chances are probably slim but it's worth a try. Or, you might be able to pay them to appear.

The launch is also a great chance to sell books. You can invite a bookshop to the launch to handle this side of things if you like, but keep in mind that you will be giving up a large percentage of your profit on each sale if you do this. For this reason, authors sometimes choose to organise book sales at the launch themselves.

Step 7: Distribution

Keep in mind that it's vital to plan your launch well and think carefully about *why* you are having it. If it's a party for friends and family, make it that; if it's a business event, run it accordingly and have a goal for how it will benefit your business. Either is fine – just don't confuse the two.

You will most likely be tempted to give copies to your close family and friends, and this is fine, but in publishing it's a bit of a tradition that friends and family buy copies from you to help support your writing and publishing venture. It's probably not cool to ask your partner or kids to buy a copy, but it's not unreasonable to expect friends to purchase copies. I've never once seen this cause a problem; the people who care about you will be more than happy to support what you are doing.

When should my book come out?

Giving some thought to the publication date of your book is important. Is it possible for you to find a date that will be relevant to your book that could help you gain publicity? For example:

- If your book is a guide to building a shed that might make a great father's day gift, release it a few weeks before father's day.
- If your book is full of holiday activities for kids, release it just before the school holidays start.
- If your book covers learning to surf, release it at the start of summer; if it's about learning to ski, release it at the start of winter.

Keep in mind that you need to give people time to buy the book, so if it's a good father's day book, don't release it *on* father's day but a few weeks before.

You need to approach the media in advance as well. Daily media needs to be approached a few days to a week in advance, weekly media at least a few weeks in advance, and monthly media at least six or eight weeks – or even more – in advance of the release date of your book.

Of course, your priority might be simply to get your book out as quickly as you can, and that's fine too. You can still use events and dates such as the above to promote your book when the time comes.

Pre-orders before the launch

Getting pre-orders for your book before it is launched can be a great way to get sales, and it also helps you manage and pay for your print run.

I've already mentioned that having your ISBN and cover as early as you can is a good idea, and obtaining pre-orders is one of the reasons. Once you have the cover, price, ISBN and some comprehensive information about your book, you can start taking orders on your website.

Because people can't actually see the book yet, it can be helpful to give them an incentive to pre-order. So, consider offering a discount or free postage, or give away one of your other products with each copy of the book.

If you have a bookshop distributor, they will also start taking pre-orders for you from bookshops before the release date.

Bookshops

Getting into bookshops can be tough as a self-published author. You can attempt to do this in two ways: DIY and using a distributor.

Step 7: Distribution

DIY bookshop distribution

Understandably, bookshops are often reluctant to deal with individual self-publishers who have only published one book and are managing the distribution themselves. They have to set up an account, order separately, and find out what the terms of trade are, all for a book that might only sell a few copies, if that. It's often just not worth the effort. But, if you are determined and have the time and energy, you can try to manage your own distribution.

The two main advantages are that you don't have to pay the cost of a distributor, and you don't have to worry about your book being accepted by a distributor. (As you would expect, you have to submit your book to a distributor for consideration. But, if you've produced a professional quality book, being accepted shouldn't be a problem.)

The cost of using a distributor is usually around 60 to 70 per cent of the RRP, but most of this actually goes to the bookshop. So if you do it yourself, you're looking at saving around 15 to 20 per cent of the RRP of your book, with 45 to 55 per cent still going to the bookshop.

If you go the DIY route, the first thing you have to do is let bookstores know that you and your book actually exist. You can do this in a number of ways:

- You can send out sample copies of your book to bookstores, along with your details and information about how they can order.

- You can visit stores and introduce yourself and your book. (Let me warn you in advance though: many bookshops will simply give you a sympathetic smile and say, 'Sorry, we don't deal with self-publishers'.)

- You can use various industry publications to announce your book, with the most prominent being the *Weekly Book Newsletter* and the monthly magazine *Books & Publishing* (both of which are excellent publications read by almost everybody in the industry).

But perhaps the best way to get your book into stores is to generate some good publicity. If you can do this, they'll be contacting you to find out how they can order. We look at publicity in Part II.

The other thing to keep in mind is that, if your book does well, it can be very time-consuming doing the distribution yourself. I recently worked with an author who had self-published her first two books and managed her own distribution very successfully, and had sold over 11,000 books over a few years, but the toll on her time was massive. Every night after work she had to deal with bookshops, package and post out books, and send and chase invoices. A few weeks after we took this distribution off her hands she told me how relieved she was and how much more free time she suddenly had. So, it's very tough to succeed with DIY and, if you *do* succeed, it will take up a lot of your time, so think long and hard before you try it.

Bookshop distribution companies

A number of excellent book distributors are available in Australia, both small and large, who will get your books into bookstores. The distributor will take the whole thing off your hands, dealing with bookshops, invoicing and sending out books.

If you want to run a professional self-publishing operation, using a distributor is a great way to go. Sure it will cost you, but trying to do it yourself and making a mess of it will cost you more. And you may only get one shot at it. Bookshops are most interested

Step 7: Distribution

in a book when it's new. If you try to do it yourself initially and it doesn't go well, you've missed your best opportunity and stores may lose interest in your book.

Some self-publishing providers offer bookshop distribution, some don't. If you use one that doesn't, this is something you will have to arrange yourself.

Ebook distribution

Ebooks are a great leveller for small publishers; you can easily make your book available worldwide, just like a larger publisher. I covered ebook distribution in detail in Step 6, but cover it again briefly here.

DIY ebook uploading

Most ebook stores allow you to upload your ebook yourself. If you have reasonable computer skills, you'll have no trouble setting up an account and uploading your files, although it can be time-consuming. Different sites have different requirements for files and information. Like most things, doing it yourself might save you a few dollars but you pay for this in the amount of time it takes. You can also use an 'aggregator' site.

Paying somebody else to do it for you

Most self-publishing service providers can handle ebook distribution for you as part of your self-publishing package.

In your business

For many more great ways to get your books to your readers and tips on how to use your book in your business, see Part II of this book.

PART II
AFTER YOUR BOOK IS PUBLISHED

Using your book in your business

Book sales

Many books and websites out there will give you the technique to 'sell a million copies of your book'; I'm sure you won't be surprised to hear that such a technique doesn't exist. Like anything in business, no sure-fire method will guarantee sales (and if such a method did exist, the people who came up with it sure wouldn't be selling it!). These promises are designed to sell books and other products for the people promoting them.

Self-publishing a book to help promote you and your business is very different from most other areas of publishing because it doesn't rely on book sales to be a success.

You must have realistic expectations about how many copies you might sell. People often have misconceptions because they only hear about best-selling books selling many thousands of copies, but nobody ever hears about the author who sold 17. The best-selling book I've ever worked on sold over 180,000 copies, but unfortunately that's the exception. The minimum viable print run for a commercial publisher is usually between 1500 and 2500 copies, depending on the book, but for self-publishers even these quantities can be difficult.

I regularly work with authors who sell 100 or 200 copies of their books and consider this a great success, because some of those book sales turned into thousands of dollars worth of work for their business. Authors self-publishing in this area very rarely make a profit solely on sales, but that's fine. They know this at the start of the project. Your book is a marketing tool, a business card, a mark of your expertise, and it sets you apart from your competitors – that's how you make money with it.

Marketing and publicity

A book is a great way to get publicity for yourself and your business. Let's say you have a marketing and publicity budget of $10,000. That could buy you a medium-sized ad in a magazine or newspaper. Or, you could use it to invest in the self-publishing of your book, and the book might get you and your business a full-page article in the same magazine, *plus* reviews and articles in ten other magazines, *and* give you all of the other benefits we're going to look at in this chapter. So, seen from a marketing and publicity perspective, a book can provide an extremely good return on investment (though you must also factor in the time invested to write the book and see it through editing and production).

Contacts

Having a book published is a great way to get in touch with people who you never really had a reason to connect with before. These can be potential or past clients, people in your industry who you'd like to get to know, people in other industries who you might like to partner with, or leaders in your field who you'd just like to let know you exist. Having a book published makes it very simple: you send them a copy! Send each copy out with a personalised cover letter, explaining you've just published this book and you thought they might be interested in it. I've regularly seen this simple approach lead to great opportunities for authors.

Lead generation

I recently spoke to an author who had carefully tracked the sales that had come to his business as a direct result of leads generated from his book. In less than six months his book had generated over $50,000 in sales!

Your book is a great way to attract the right clients to your business. When people ring up your company and make enquiries, offer to send them a copy of your book (that's what I plan to do with this book!). Your book will contain all the information your potential clients need to find a service provider. No doubt you're excellent at what you do, and in your book you've told people what to look for. From your book people will gain an idea of what you do and how you do it, and they will also gain some insight into your personality and how you work. From this, they will decide whether you are the right person for them or not. The people who have read your book and then contacted you are much more likely to become clients, and those who decide not to contact you were probably never right for you anyway.

Give your book away

You can use your book as a giveaway for potential clients. This is very powerful and something many authors do. You can do this in all sorts of ways:

- When somebody contacts your business with an enquiry, send them a copy of the book.

- Use it as an incentive for people to buy from you, or to purchase a larger amount.

- Send a copy to past clients you haven't spoken to in a while, just to remind them you are there.

Sample chapters

Many authors give away a free sample of their book on their website, which is a great use of the book. Not only will it attract people to your site, it will also generate book sales, as many people will want to buy the whole book after reading the sample.

Speaking engagements

I had an author recently who secured a speaking engagement at a major institute just days after sending them a copy of his book. Publishing a book will do this. Even in these days of the internet, blogs, YouTube, Facebook and Twitter, being a published author still carries a great deal of cachet and credibility.

Another accountant I worked with a number of years ago said that after he published his first book he noticed that his appointments on average started getting a little shorter. It took him a while to figure out why. He'd written a book about taxation, and it was displayed in the foyer of his office so clients could see it when they came in. He realised that ever since the book had been displayed clients were accepting his advice just a little more quickly and as a result his appointments were getting just a bit shorter. The extra credibility the book had given him meant his clients held him in higher regard and accepted his advice more quickly and easily. He has since written four more books.

Articles and blogs

Having a book published gives you the authority to write about your industry, and this can lead to articles and blogs.

You can write a few articles based on the content of your book and send them around to relevant outlets for possible publication. Having had a book published increases your chances of being accepted. (Have a look at the bios of articles you read; you'll quite often see that the author of the article has also written a book on the same topic.)

The book itself can also be a source of articles. You can pull out, say, 1000 words, and then tweak this extract a little to turn it into a standalone article. This can usually be done simply by adding a new introduction and conclusion, and removing any material that would be out of context in an article. Or, you can simply offer extracts of the book for publication – this is quite common.

Keep in mind that media outlets are always hungry for content. Now that you have a book you will be of great interest to them, and you now also have the authority to comment on your industry.

Book reviews

One of the first things you should do when you receive stock of your book from the printer is send out review copies. You should be prepared for this a few weeks before the books arrive, so that you can get onto it as soon as they come in.

You can do a basic media mail-out yourself, or you can pay a publicist as part of a media campaign. Enlisting a publicist can cost anywhere from $500 to $5000, or even more. If you put in a bit of effort, you should be able to do a reasonable job of it yourself; however, if media exposure is an essential part of the plan for your book, paying a publicist will be money well spent.

If you're going the DIY approach, you need to prepare two key components:

- a media release
- a media list.

A media release is basically a one-page summary of your book, to be included with the book when you send it out. A lot of information is available about how to write a good media release so I won't go into too much detail, but here's a few tips:

- Make it only one page. Journos are very busy people and don't want to look through a 15-page media kit.
- Write your release like an article, so the journalist can just publish it as is.
- Make sure you include all the key info about your book, such as the price, where it can be purchased, when it was released and the ISBN. Also include your contact details, including phone numbers (mobile and landline) and your email address, and offer yourself for interview.

Using your book in your business

- Tailor your media release for each outlet. For example, if you've written a book about sharemarket investing, your media release for *Shares* magazine might focus on the technical aspects of what you do, while your media release for *The Age* might focus on how everyday investors can get the most out of the sharemarket. Make sure each release still accurately reflects the content of your book.

- Try to make it topical. So, with a sharemarket book, study how the market has performed recently and tie this into your media release. This gives journalists an angle for a story.

- Include a few quotes from you about your subject. These give the journalists something they can easily pull out of the media release if they wish.

You can purchase media lists, but if you're willing to spend some time surfing the net and on the phone you can put together a decent media list yourself. You should be able to find 100 media outlets to send your book to without too much trouble. That might sound like a lot, but if you consider newspapers, magazines, blogs, websites, television and radio, it's actually quite easy. You can sometimes send two copies just to one newspaper: if you've written a book about healthy eating for kids, you can send one copy to the book editor and one to the health editor.

You can prepare a media list almost entirely from the internet these days. Here are some outlets for you to look into:

- Newspapers. Send a copy to the books editor and to the editor relevant to your topic. So, the real estate editor if you've written a property book, the food editor if you've written a cook book and the fiction editor if you've written a book about honest politicians.

- Magazines that cover your area, including industry mags.
- Websites and blogs that cover your industry. You can offer to write guest blogs.
- Radio and television. Do your homework and find radio and television programs that cover your subject. Don't forget about local radio.
- Local newspapers: tailor a media release specifically for your local paper, concentrating on how you and your business contribute to the local community.

Here are some tips for preparing your media list:

- Wherever possible, get the name of a contact person you can send to. This is very important, firstly because it increases the chances of the book reaching the right person, and secondly because following up will be much easier.
- You should be able to find most contact details online. For any that you can't, give the company a call.
- Send the book to an assistant editor rather than the editor. The assistant is usually the person who opens and sorts through the mail, and presents anything of interest to the editor.
- If you're trying to get your book picked up by a radio program, send the book to the producers of the program, not the on-air presenter.
- If you've made a decent effort and still can't find a contact name, use the title of the person you'd like to receive the book; for example, if you're trying to get onto the Richard Stubbs program on 774, address the book to 'The Producer: Richard Stubbs program'.

Using your book in your business

Before you send your books out to the media, here are a few things to have handy:

- A low-resolution and high-resolution JPG of your cover, which contacts will likely ask for if they write a review. Print publications will want the hi-res; online outlets will usually want the low-res.
- A PDF copy of the media release, to email to them in case they've lost it.
- Some article ideas that you can pitch if you get into a discussion with a journalist.
- Some interesting facts and figures about yourself and your business that you can use in a discussion with a journalist.

After you've sent out your books, you need to follow up. This can be done by phone or email. The first thing is to confirm that the person did in fact receive the book. It's not uncommon for the books to end up sitting on an assistant's desk, or to be in a pile of 50 books in the corner, or – especially in large organisations such as newspapers – to have simply disappeared into a vortex, never to be seen again. If the contact hasn't received the book, offer to send another one. If they have, the next step is to ask them if they're interested in doing anything with it.

It will be up to you to judge each exchange; if the person on the other end of the phone or email is quite emphatically not interested, it's usually best to accept this and move onto the next one. You don't win any friends being pushy. But you might receive a response along the lines of 'We're looking at it' or 'Yes, we liked it and we might use it if we do a story on that topic'. If you feel comfortable doing so, ask them if you can provide any more information, or if they would like to interview you, or perhaps offer some article ideas that relate to your book.

As a business card

A book makes a great business card. Make sure you always have a few in your car, and always take some to meetings, industry events, seminars, or... anywhere! When everybody else is swapping business cards, hand out a few copies of your book! Don't be afraid to give away copies. Consider it a marketing expense. I recently had an author who printed 2500 copies of his book and was giving away 2000 of these. This was his third book, and he knew the value of complimentary copies. His book was about property, and I recently saw him on the cover (yes, the cover) of two property investment magazines.

Qualify clients

A book is a great way to qualify your clients. A strong business is not built just on attracting a large number of clients but also on attracting a large number of the *right* clients.

Giving a copy of your book to potential clients is a great way to introduce them to what you do and how you do it, and therefore increase the chances that you'll attract the right clients. Potential clients will gain a good feel for you and your business, and this will help them decide if you're right for them. Your book can also include practical information such as time lines and prices, which will further filter clients. For example, in writing this book I've done my best to reflect the way I do business. I give my clients the best information I can. I don't try to 'sell' them on self-publishing, just inform them. I present people with the relevant information and let them decide for themselves. Many people who come to me have already made the decision and just want information.

You can even include a page at the back of the book, encouraging clients to contact you. (Don't make this seem too much like an ad. People don't want to be sold to in a book. If your book is great and the client believes you can meet their needs, they will contact you.)

Stand out in your industry

If I could sum up the benefits of writing a book for your business, it would be that it will make you stand out. All of the other benefits you receive will flow from this simple fact. Chances are most others in your industry have not written a book, and possibly nobody has.

Writing a book gives you authority. It presents you as an expert. It also reflects well on you personally. Writing a book takes time, effort and commitment, and these are qualities potential clients will appreciate.

Don't go the 'hard sell'

You don't need to have a hard-sell approach in your book. The best way to sell yourself and your business is to write an excellent book that will meet the needs of your clients, and to produce it professionally. This will give clients the information they need and will reflect well on your business. It will establish you as an expert and leader in your field. It will set you apart from the competition. You don't need to do any more selling than that.

I've seen authors who have gone the hard sell in their books; they've mentioned their business or their website at every chance, and included ads (plural) at the back. I've never seen this make any difference, and it may well turn people off. Do you really think readers who are looking for your service and have been impressed by your book are *not* going to contact you? And, as we looked at earlier, this helps qualify your clients. The ones who don't contact you after reading your book have decided you can't help them and so most likely wouldn't have come to you anyway!

Don't worry about giving 'too much' info away

Authors who are writing a book for their business are often concerned about giving away 'too much' information in their book. They're concerned about giving away trade secrets, or that if they give away too much detail people then won't need their services.

I can understand this concern, but worrying about this is unnecessary. With the obvious exception of giving away proprietary information that is important to your business, I believe the best way to go is to give your readers as much information as you can. They'll appreciate this, and they will still most definitely need your services. I haven't held back anything in this book, but reading it hasn't turned you into a publisher, editor or designer. You by now should have an excellent idea of what's involved in self-publishing your book, have some valuable information to help you make decisions, and have a good indication of how much you might pay and how long it might take. *But*, you still have to find people to help you with your book. That hasn't changed; now, however, you have the information you need to do that. Giving you as much information as I can hasn't reduced your need to get help with your book at all, and the same will be true for your readers.

So, with the exception of your company's secret sauce, give away as much information as you can. Your readers will value your information and be much more likely to come to you than if you scrimp on the useful stuff in an effort to make them sign up with you to get the info they really need.

Other stuff

PLR/ELR

PLR stands for Public Lending Rights, and ELR stands for Educational Lending Rights. PLR and ELR is money paid to authors to compensate them for their books being used in public and school libraries. You can find the forms to apply for these schemes at arts.gov.au/literature/lending_rights. As a self-publisher you will have to complete the forms for both the publisher and author.

The schemes conduct surveys of the numbers of books borrowed from libraries and pay authors accordingly. Minimum thresholds need to be reached before you'll receive a payment. Many authors don't receive anything because their books aren't borrowed enough, but it's still worth applying. You may get nothing out of it, but you may get a cheque in the mail for $250 when you least expect it, and who wouldn't like that?

CAL

CAL stands for Copyright Agency Limited. CAL has a scheme that pays authors when their material is photocopied or licensed for use, usually to schools, universities or government agencies.

As with PLR/ELR, minimum thresholds need to be met before payments are made, but again it's worth participating because you just may receive an unexpected cheque in the mail one day.

Legal Deposit

Copyright law in Australia requires that you submit a copy of your book to the National Library and your state library for archiving. In the publishing industry these are usually simply called 'library copies'; the proper name for this is Legal Deposit. This needs to be done as soon as your book is released.

If you have purchased an ISBN and don't submit copies of your book to the libraries, you will receive a letter from the libraries asking where your book is. You don't want annoyed librarians chasing you, so don't forget to submit your books!

At the time of writing, the National Library doesn't legally require submission of ebooks but does accept voluntary submissions. Some state libraries do require submission of ebooks, so check the requirements in your state.

My Identifiers

My Identifiers is a website of Thorpe-Bowker, on which publishers buy ISBNs and barcodes and list details of their titles. You can sign up for this yourself if you like, but if you're using a self-publishing service provider they should be able to do this for you.

Other stuff

Once your book is listed on this service it shows up on the Books in Print database, which is one of the two major databases bookshops use to order from publishers. (The other is called Title Page; this is rarely used by smaller publishers or self-publishers because it is prohibitively expensive.)

Appendix: your questions answered

Some of the following issues are addressed throughout this book, but I've answered some common questions here for easy reference.

Which is better: traditional publishing, partnership publishing or self-publishing?

This question is easy to answer: they are all good! It's all a matter of which best suits your aims for your book.

In the particular niche of publishing for small business, self-publishing is often the preferred option. There are a number of reasons for this:

- You don't have to worry about whether your book will be accepted by a publisher. If you've written a novel you might be happy to spend 12 months trying to get your book picked up by a publisher, but if you've written your book for your business that time equals potential forgone profits.
- As it's a business expense, and so an investment in their business, self-publishers in this area are more comfortable spending money.

- When you self-publish, no restrictions whatsoever are put on what else you can do with the material, such as using it in a blog, putting a free sample on your website or writing an article. If you have a contract with a publisher, they will most likely put some restriction on what you can do with the material in the book. (This is not unreasonable, as the publisher has paid to produce the book and must protect their investment.)
- You can use the book exactly how you want to in your business without any obligations to a publisher.

How long will it take to produce my book?

For a book of around 40,000 words the whole process from completion of the manuscript to having printed books usually takes two to three months, with wrapping up the ebook and uploading it usually finished a few weeks after this. Of course, some projects can take longer for a number of reasons. Most self-publishers are producing their book while still working in their day job, so it can take a while for them to check proofs and so on.

If you need your book completed urgently, have a chat to your service provider. For an extra fee they might be able to fast-track your book.

A more detailed breakdown of how long each step usually takes is provided in Step 1.

Can self-publishing lead to a deal with a major publisher?

It certainly can! It's not common but it does happen. If you've done really well with your self-publishing project and would like to see what else you can do with your book, you could consider approaching a publisher. They may not be interested in re-publishing your book as is, but they might be interested in a second edition.

When should I do a second edition? How much needs to be changed?

No strict rules exist about when you should do a second edition (if you do) and how much needs to change. Usually 12 or 18 months after the first edition is a reasonable time frame. This will renew interest in your book and provide you with more opportunities to build your profile and promote your business.

I have a rule of thumb about how much needs to change for a second edition: if I own the first edition of a book, will buying the second edition be worthwhile? If the answer is no, there wasn't much point releasing a second edition. As a general rule, I think you need to change at least one-third of the content *and* update the rest of the book to make a second edition worthwhile.

What are CMYK and RGB?

These are two different colour 'models'. CMYK stands for 'Cyan, Magenta, Yellow, Black' (black is 'K' – various theories exist as to why), and RGB stands for 'Red, Green, Blue'. You don't need to know too much about these, except that CMYK is used for printed books and RGB is used for computers and the internet. Any images you include in your printed book must be CMYK. If they aren't, your printer will most likely send your file back to you and ask you to fix it up.

Your designer, editor or self-publishing service provider will be able to help you if you have supplied images in the wrong colour mode.

What resolution do my images need to be for printing?

As with colour modes, printing and computers have different resolution requirements. To get good quality on a computer screen an image only needs to be 72 dpi (dots per inch), but to get good quality in print an image needs to be 300 dpi. Complicated formulas are actually involved in working out the best resolution, depending on the printing specs you're using, but 300 dpi has become the default minimum setting for good-quality printing of images, so use this as your standard. (Working out the resolution is also not as simple as just giving the DPI, but in 99.9 per cent of cases it is enough so I'm not going to get all technical here.)

For this reason, you need to be careful downloading something from the internet; it may look fine on your screen or on your bubble jet printer at home but it might not look so good in your book. As somewhat of a paradox, the higher resolution of a book actually means an image may look worse. This doesn't mean you can't use images from the internet, just that you have to be aware of the potential limitations. And, as discussed in Step 2, if you do download an image, make sure you obtain permission to use it!

How long should my book be?

The minimum viable length for a book for your business is around 30,000 words, which is around 80 to 100 pages in Microsoft Word. Many variables affect how long your book will be when formatted and printed, but generally 30,000 words will turn into a book of about 160 to 180 pages. The average length of books we work on is around 40,000 to 50,000 words, though a book of 100,000 words or more isn't uncommon, which is fine as long as it's 100,000 words of useful information. This book is about 35,000

Appendix: your questions answered

words long. A longer book will increase most of the costs of self-publishing your book.

How much should I charge for my book?

This is a very common question for first-time self-publishers. You need to consider a number of issues:

- What are similar books selling for? Go to your local bookshops and surf the net to find out. (It's always a good idea to go to a bookshop if you can, so you can get an idea of the look and feel of the books, and have a look through them. You're not just looking at a screen.)
- Is it better to sell more books at a lower price or fewer books at a higher price?
- Where is the book going to be positioned in the market? If your book is for company CEOs, you can probably sell it for more – they might even be suspicious of your book if it's cheap! But if you've written a book about how to pay your mortgage off more quickly, chances are your buyers are looking to save money.
- Is your book highly specialised? If very few – or no – direct competitors exist for your book, you can probably charge more.
- What were the production costs of your book? These need to be taken into consideration.
- Will you be doing an ebook, and if so how much will you be selling this for?

While taking all of the above into consideration is important, I think the best guide is what other comparable books are selling for. This is what the market is telling other publishers to price their books at – you should charge more only if you have a good reason to do so.

Glossary

advance copies (advances): the first few copies off the press that are sent by the printer to the publisher for approval, before the bulk stock is delivered. These need to be checked carefully for print quality.

advance royalty payment: payment made to an author by a publisher upon signing a contract. As the name suggests, it is an advance payment on royalties yet to be earned. Let's say an author is paid an advance of $1000, and then the first royalty payment due to the author after six months of sales is $1500. This author will only be paid $500, as they have already received $1000. If the author doesn't make enough sales to cover the advance they are not usually required to pay it back. This is a risk the publisher takes. There have been cases recently of authors being taken to court over advance payments when the author has accepted the payment but then failed to complete the manuscript.

bleeds: the extra printing that goes over the trim size of the book. Because exactly aligning printing with the edge of a page isn't possible, books are printed on pages slightly larger than needed with the printing going over the edge of the required size, and then the book is trimmed down to size. This ensures that the printing goes all the way to the edge of the page.

CIP: Cataloguing in Publication – the National Library catalogue entry for your book.

crop marks: the small marks that define the corners of the page of a book. The proofs you receive from your editor, designer or printer may have crop marks. If you'd like to get an idea of how your book will look when it is trimmed to size, you can print out a few pages of these proofs, rule between the crops marks, and then trim or fold the pages along these lines. This will give you the trimmed size of your book and a better idea of how your pages will look.

digital printing: a method of printing used to print smaller quantities of books, usually up to around 1000 copies. A digital press looks like a very large photocopier.

DRM: digital rights management – the electronic protection applied to ebook files in an effort to stop piracy, often with only limited success.

EPUB: electronic publication – the most common ebook format.

GSM (or gm^2): grams per square metre – the weight of the paper your book is printed on. The interior is usually printed on stock around 80 GSM, and covers on 250 to 300 GSM. Higher GSM stock is usually, though not always, thicker.

Glossary

hand unload (or 'trolley unload'): if you've printed a large quantity and your books are being delivered to your home, you must tell the printer you don't have a forklift and that you require 'hand unload'; otherwise, they may assume they're sending the books to a warehouse and that you have a forklift. If this happens they might send a large semi-trailer that can't fit down your street, and you won't get your books! 'Hand unload' may also affect the cost of delivery.

ISBN: international standard book number – the number allocated to *each version* of your book. For example, an EPUB, MOBI, paperback and hardback version of your book each require a different ISBN.

ISSN: international standard serial number – used for magazines and books that are regularly updated as part of a series. An ISSN is rarely used for a book.

MOBI: the Amazon ebook format.

offset printing: a method of printing that uses large presses to print large quantities of books, usually around 1000 copies or more.

PDF: portable document format – an Adobe format. This format allows files to be moved from one computer to another without causing formatting problems. This makes it the ideal format for supplying files to the printer, and also for giving away electronic samples of your book; for example, on your website.

perfect binding: the most common form of book binding, where pages are glued into the cover of the book. Think of it as 'standard' book binding.

permission request: the request to a copyright owner to use their material in your book.

proofs: a version of your book (text and cover) at various stages in its production. Proofs may be supplied in electronic or hard copy format. You'll receive instructions from your editor, designer, printer or whoever sent you the proofs about what is required of you. Some stages are a chance for you to make changes, while other proofs are simply to sign off your approval; for example, the final set of proofs before your book goes to the printer.

print on demand: a process whereby small quantities of books are printed only when the book has been purchased by a customer. Usually used for quantities from one to one hundred copies. Sites such as Amazon use this method for many of the books they sell.

royalties: payments made by a publisher to an author for sales of a book. Royalty rates are usually around 10 per cent of the recommended retail price of the book.

saddle stitching: a common form of binding for shorter books, such as picture books. The pages are stapled together with large staples. Saddle stitched books do not have a spine.

sheet-fed printing: a form of offset printing that uses large, individual sheets of paper rather than rolls, and provides slightly more accurate printing. Web presses (which use rolls of paper) are usually used for single-colour printing, while sheet fed is usually used for colour because the alignment of the inks is better. Sheet-fed printing is more expensive than web printing.

Glossary

spine width: the width of your spine, which you need to obtain from your printer once your page extent is finalised.

stock: the paper your book is printed on. You should discuss your book with your printer to ensure you get the right paper.

tracked changes: a very useful feature of Microsoft Word that allows you to see and then approve or reject changes that have been made to your book by your editor, and allows your editor to also see any further changes you make.

trim size: the size of your book after it has been bound and trimmed. There are common book formats and it's usually a good idea to use one of these. For example, novels are often printed 129 mm wide by 198 mm high (usually written as 129 × 198), and a common non-fiction size is 130 × 250. Trim sizes are usually expressed as width × height (though sometimes they're given as height × width, so make sure you confirm what size is being referred to). Different printers may use sizes that vary by a few millimetres.

trolley unload *see* 'hand unload'.

typesetting: the process of laying out the interior of your book, done by a designer or a typesetter.

unit cost: The cost of each individual book. Unit cost doesn't usually include editing, layout and other costs, although you can calculate this if you wish.

web printing: web printing is a form of offset printing that uses very large rolls of paper fed through a press. When the paper is threaded through the press it looks like a web, hence the name.

Index

A
advance copies 85–87
Amazon 54, 65
articles 115
authors' rights 15

B
back cover 60–62
barcodes 55–56, 61
blogs 115
blurb 60–61
book launches 101–104
book reviews 116–120
books
—delivery of 87–88
—for business promotion 21, 111–123
—length of 132–133
—mistakes in 46, 88–89
—number of copies sold 111–112
—price of 61, 94–95, 133–134
—size of 64–65
bookshops 104–107
Books in Print 127

C
Cataloguing in Publication (CIP) 56
CMYK 131
colour models 131
copyediting 41–46
copyright 47–51
Copyright Agency Limited (CAL) 126
cover design 6, 28, 57–63
—ebooks and 62–63

D
defamatory material 51–52
developmental editing 40–41
digital printing 75–76
digital rights management (DRM) 98–100
distribution 7, 101–107

E
ebook aggregators 96–97
ebooks 7, 62–63, 91–100
 —distribution of 96–98, 107
 —file formats 91–94
 —formatting 28
 —price of 94–95, 133–134
 —uploading 28, 96–98, 107
editing 6, 28, 33–56
 —stages of 38–46
editors
 —need for 34–35
 —role of 35–38
Educational Lending Rights (ELR) 125
EPUB 92–93

F
first edit 41–44

I
image resolution 132
indexing 6, 28, 71–72
 —ebooks and 72, 95

interior design 6, 28, 63–64
 —doing it yourself 65–66
ISBNs 52–55
 —Amazon and 54

L
lamination 84
lead generation 113–114
Legal Deposit 126

M
major publishers 130–131
manuscript assessment 39
marketing 112
Microsoft Publisher 67
Microsoft Word 42–43, 67
MOBI 93
My Identifiers 126–127

N
National Library of Australia 56, 126

O
offset printing 74–75

P
paper 83–84
partnership publishing 17–19, 129–130
PDF 93–94
planning 6, 13–32

Index

printers 78–81
printing 7, 28, 32, 65–67, 73–89
   —importance of 73–74
   —types of 74–78
print on demand (POD) 65, 76–77
professional-quality books 5
project management 23–32
proofreading 6, 28, 46, 69–71
proofs 84–85
public domain 48–49
publicity 112
Public Lending Rights (PLR) 125
publishing models 13–19, 129–130

R

reprints 88–89
RGB 131

S

sample chapters 114
second edit 45–46
second editions 131
sections 65–66
self-publishing 16–17, 129–130
   —assembling your team 23–25
   —cost of 20–21, 30–32
   —getting started 3–4
   —managing yourself 23–32
   —pros and cons of 19–22
   —reasons for 4–5
   —timeframes for 27–30, 130–131
self-publishing companies 24–25
   —choosing 37–38
seven-step self-publishing system 6–8, 13–107
speaking engagements 114–115
spine 60–62, 82–83
standing out from the crowd 8–9, 121

T

Thorpe-Bowker 126–127
Title Page 127
tracked changes 43
traditional publishing 14–16, 129–130
typos 46

U

unit cost 81–82

W

writing 5

mhpublishing.com.au

Australia's #1 in self-publishing for small business

www.ingramcontent.com/pod-product-compliance
Lightning Source LLC
Chambersburg PA
CBHW071436160426
43195CB00013B/1926